Boys to Men

Teens Write About Manhood

By Youth Communication

Edited by Al Desetta

YOUTH COMMUNICATION

True Stories by Teens

Boys to Men

EXECUTIVE EDITORS
Keith Hefner and Laura Longhine

CONTRIBUTING EDITORS
Philip Kay, Clarence Haynes, Hope Vanderberg, Katia Hetter,
Kendra Hurley, Laura Longhine, Marie Glancy, and Nora McCarthy

LAYOUT & DESIGN
Efrain Reyes, Jr. and Jeff Faerber

COVER ART
Phillip Rolano

For reprint information, please contact Youth Communication.

ISBN 978-1-933939-73-5

Second, Expanded Edition

Printed in the United States of America

Youth Communication ®
New York, New York
www.youthcomm.org

Table of Contents

Contents

Contents

Contents

Introduction

What does it mean to be a man? This is an especially difficult question nowadays, when boys often lack positive role models and are bombarded with contradictory messages about appropriate behavior.

Boys to Men collects 18 true stories by teens, who write about crucial moments in their lives that helped them make the transition to maturity and manhood. They touch upon a wide range of experiences and viewpoints.

Ferentz Lafargue recalls playing baseball, football, and manhunt with his childhood friends Devon, John, and Angel in a parking lot behind a store in their neighborhood.

"There weren't any me's or I's in the parking lot," Ferentz recalls. "We were a team."

But while Ferentz stayed in school and stayed away from trouble, his three friends, all of them smart and talented, ended up involved in crime and drugs. And Ferentz wonders why they made such different choices. "These days the parking lot is just used for parking cars. We don't even keep in touch like we used to," he writes. "The only thing we have in common anymore is that we grew up."

The anonymous author of "Am I the Father?" experiences anger and fear after a girl accuses him of getting her pregnant. Even though the writer doesn't have a dime to his name, and isn't even sure the child is his, he starts planning to be a father.

"If it was mine," he writes, "I wasn't going to abandon it...I knew the pain of growing up without a dad, and I always swore I wouldn't do that if I had a child. I would have to stop acting like a boy and take care of my responsibilities as a man."

All the writers go through similar rites of passage. When Michael Orr witnesses a fellow foster care resident get discharged to a homeless shelter, he starts making a plan for his future. Chris Kanarick freezes with stage fright at his Bar Mitzvah and can't recite from the Torah, but then gets control of himself and becomes a man in the eyes of the Jewish religion—"A man who had just embarrassed himself in front of friends and family," he writes, "but a man nonetheless." Divine Strickland decides to stop trying to mask his gay identity. Daniel Verzhbo strives to rebuild a relationship with his mother after losing himself in crime and drugs.

Abandoned by his father, Rashad Evans steps up to be a father figure to his little brother and vows not to make the same mistake when he has children. "As I see it, my father is far from a man. A man takes care of his responsibilities. A man owns up to his mistakes and tries his best to correct them. A man doesn't give up on raising a child before he even starts."

Many of these stories challenge traditional notions of masculinity. Troy Shawn Welcome, accustomed to being in control around the opposite sex, is unsettled when a girl aggressively approaches him on the street. Jonathan Maseng fears being teased for being an opera singer, but when his friends find out they encourage and support him. Tyrone Vaden has been raised in tough neighborhoods, but understands that a real man doesn't have to resort to violence to get respect.

Boys to Men will prompt teens of both genders to think hard about male roles, behavior, and stereotypes, and provides positive examples of young men coming to terms with their identities.

In the following stories, names and/or identifying details have been changed: *The Crew from the Parking Lot, Becoming the Man My Dad Couldn't Be, Am I the Father?, From Shy Guy to Smooth Talker, My Boy Wanted a Boyfriend,* and *Messing Around's No Match for Love.*

Hugo Tamashiro

The Crew from the Parking Lot

By Ferentz Lafargue

The parking lot behind Wertheimer's department store was once a place where boyhood dreams were born. Dreams of growing up and playing for the Yankees or Giants someday, dreams of meeting that girl, the one you knew was out there, the one who was made for you. My friends and I used to spend the whole afternoon there playing baseball, football, manhunt, and practically anything else you could think of.

One day we noticed a piece of wood in the corner of the lot. We found a rock to prop it up and made ourselves a bicycle ramp. We practiced jumping for a week or two until the wood broke and it was back to playing bike tag and waiting for the next thing to come along.

Every winter there would be huge piles of snow in the corners of the lot. We would start out by doing some light skiing to get warmed up and soften up the snow. (The skis were made of the finest cardboard we could find.) But we all know what happens when you put a bunch of guys somewhere with snow... SNOWFIGHT!!

The rules were simple: whichever mountain you were on was your territory, and whoever was with you was your team. We would fight until one team captured the other team's mountain or the teams split up and it was every man for himself. We would go home looking like we had just climbed Mount Everest, and sometimes I think that would have been easier.

We also shared a lot of disappointments in the parking lot. We felt bad for Ed when he didn't make the varsity basketball team. We felt sorry when Devon's girl Wendy moved away. (They were the royal couple of the parking lot.) When Abner and Carlos were sent to fight in Iraq, we all kept an eye on the news. There weren't any "me's" or "I's" in the parking lot—we were a team.

But these days the parking lot is just used for parking cars. We don't even keep in touch like we used to. Rarely will you see two of us together. Some have moved away. The rest just feel like they're miles away. At least to me they do. The only thing we have in common anymore is that we grew up.

When I look around now and see people that I used to be down with back in the days, I feel really sorry for some of those guys.

Devon was the superstar of the parking lot. He could throw, run, catch—the whole nine. We used to think he was the total package. We thought he would play high school baseball or football, then get drafted or get a scholarship, and go on to become a major leaguer. But instead of going out for one of the teams, he opted to be down with the fellas, hanging out and doing things like robbing people, stealing chains, or getting caught up in stupid gang battles.

Now he's one of the people who comes up to me and talks about how he messed up, how he should have stayed in school.

Now the only things he strives for are his own apartment, a GED, a job, and a car. Devon's only 18 and has been sent to the jail on Riker's Island two times already. The sad thing is he has no fear of going back.

Devon's younger brother John was a pretty good ballplayer too, but more importantly he was a B+ student and a born leader. He was never afraid of being team captain. In fact, he thrived on it. He used to talk about joining the Marines and getting his M-14. Now John is 17 and has a kid and is not even close to a high school diploma. He was hardly ever in school last year. The word is that John is dealing guns. An M-14 is probably child's play compared to some of the guns he's come in contact with.

Then there's Angel. Angel used to be my best friend and in a way he always will be. Angel had drive and determination.

The only thing Angel seems determined to do is mess up his life.

One summer he lost his glove and, since he was the only lefty in the parking lot, he had no one to lend him one. But Angel decided not to let that keep him on the sidelines. He found a right-handed glove and for about a year and a half he tried to be right-handed. He started doing almost everything right-handed.

Eventually he got another left-handed glove. But even after that you could occasionally see him tricking an opposing batter with a wicked right-handed curve ball. Angel hasn't dropped out yet, not officially, but I doubt he goes to school more than five full days a year. When he does go he usually cuts out early in the day. Now Angel's dealing drugs. He used to have determination, but these days the only thing Angel seems determined to do is mess up his life.

The sad thing is that these are the guys that little kids look up to. The other day one of my friends and I were walking down 89th Avenue and one of my little brother's friends came up to us with a fake blunt that he had rolled up, and he was telling us how good it was. This kid is 10 years old at most. But you really can't blame him. That's what he sees around him. That's what's considered cool.

The ones who plan to go on to college leave the neighborhood as soon as they've finished high school and have some money in the bank. They want to move as far away as they can, as fast as they can.

Then there's me. I was the youngest kid in the parking lot, which meant I was last to get picked for the teams and the first to get picked on. I was like everyone's little brother. I just stood back and watched everyone else. I looked up to those guys. But I knew who they really were. I was smart enough to learn from their mistakes.

It's almost like I'm their last hope of success

They still keep an eye out for me. Every time one of them hears about me doing anything good, he's always ready to congratulate me and tell me to keep it up. It's almost like I'm their last hope of success—if I come out OK, then they'll honestly be able to say they had a hand in raising me.

I intend to go to college and study communications and advertising. One day, hopefully, I'll be writing for a big-time newspaper or working for an advertising company. Then I'd like to help fix up my neighborhood and do whatever I can to help out some of my old friends. But whatever I end up doing, one thing I won't do is let those guys down and mess up my life.

Remembering all those good times we had in the parking lot was enough to make me cry. I hope everyone has a parking lot in their lives. What good is a tree without roots?

*Ferentz was 16 when he wrote this story.
He later attended Queens College and Yale University,
and became a professor of literature at Eugene Lang College.*

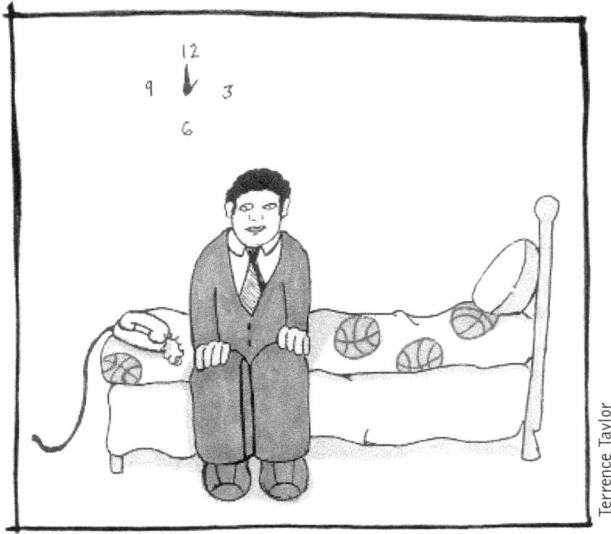

Terrence Taylor

Becoming the Man
My Dad Couldn't Be

By Rashad Evans

One day in February I decided to go onto my MySpace account, which I hadn't checked in a while. When I signed in, I noticed I had a new friend request and a new message. I looked at the message first. The "From" line said "Jones" and it didn't hit me right away who it was. The message said something like: "I knew I would find you on MySpace. I understand if you don't want to talk to me but I hope we can talk."

At first I thought it was a girl and I was confused because I didn't know a girl with the last name Jones. I went to my new friend request next. I saw the same mysterious person and I accepted their friendship request. Then I clicked on the profile. That's when it hit me in the face, real hard. It was Walter Jones, my "father."

My father left when I was a baby and my mom rarely talked about him. All I knew was that he used to live in New York City with his mother and now he lived in Delaware. Growing up, I only remember seeing him four times. Each time he visited, he made it seem that he was here to stay by talking about the things that we were going to do together, like playing basketball and creating rap songs. Then he'd disappear for years. I can't even remember the last time I saw him, maybe when I was 7 years old, maybe when I was 10.

I'd wonder from time to time what my life would've been like if my father had stayed with the family. I felt we would've been better off financially. My mother wouldn't have had all the pressure to provide for my brother and me, and we might have had more time together as a family.

Sometimes I'd daydream about being with my father, going together to catch a basketball game or playing at the park. But eventually I would come back to Earth, and I was still the child with no father.

I knew I had a father figure in John and he wasn't going to up and leave anytime soon.

I had a great mother, but felt that only a man could teach me how to be a man. When I was about 13, I found myself constantly looking for male role models. For some reason, I knew I needed male influences around me.

Every chance I got I'd tag along with my cousin Rob, who's eight years older than me, and mimic everything he did that seemed man-like. He would puff out his chest and I would do the same. He would talk to a girl and I'd try that too. It worked while I was with him, but he lived in Bushwick and I lived in Crown Heights, a different neighborhood in Brooklyn, so I didn't see him that often. I wanted to find a father figure who was close and who I could really learn from.

That search led me to my neighbor John. He was about 10

years older than me, so by the time I was 13 he was already a man of 23. He was tall, a great athlete, and he stayed out of trouble. I thought he was the perfect guy to be around.

One day when I was 13 and my little brother Kevin was 11, I took some money from my mother's drawer to buy Chinese food. Kevin said he wanted no part of it, which was unusual since he was usually the troublemaker. I bought my food, ate it, and left the evidence in my brother's room.

When my mother came home and noticed her money was missing, I immediately blamed Kevin. She believed me because he had a reputation for lying and I didn't. Kevin felt so betrayed by me that he ran away from home that night.

When we realized he was gone, around midnight, we panicked. I called John right away because I knew he'd help me. John and I looked all over for my brother and all night he kept reassuring me we were going to find him. Whenever he saw me start to worry, he'd crack a joke. I could see in his eyes and by the way that he was walking that he was extremely tired, but he did what a father would do and stayed by my side. It made me feel like John was there to stay.

It was so dark and all I could think were the worst thoughts. When we came across a cemetery, it felt like we hadn't come upon it by coincidence and I couldn't help but cry. But within a couple of seconds, I stopped. Not because I got over it that quickly, but because I suddenly noticed that this big, strong, tough man was crying right beside me. I felt like John felt my pain, and I no longer felt as bad. After that day, I knew I had a father figure in John and he wasn't going to up and leave anytime soon.

Eventually we found Kevin walking around the block and he looked happy to see us. I apologized to him and he forgave me, because he saw how much I cared about bringing him back home.

That night, I learned that I wasn't the only one in need of a father figure. A couple of weeks after running away, my brother started acting out more and more frequently. He was disrespectful to his teachers and he was getting into fights almost every day.

While my father hadn't been around at all, my brother's father came in and out of his life every two years or so. My mother and I eventually came to the conclusion that he was acting out because he was so hurt about his father promising to be there and then leaving again. That's when I realized that my brother needed a father figure and, like me, he needed one who was nearby. So I put myself in that role.

I told Kevin that if there was ever anything he wanted to talk about, I'd have his back. I began helping him with homework and I did fun things with him, too. He especially enjoyed our trips to the park and the video game store. I did my best to help him like a real father would.

I could see changes in my little brother's behavior almost immediately. He stopped doing sneaky things like stealing money from my drawer and he no longer started fights in school. My mother was grateful for all my efforts and she always thanked me. I could tell Kevin appreciated it, too, because he would always refer to me as his father figure and we became closer than ever.

I realized that my brother needed a father figure, so I put myself in that role.

Over the next couple of years, I got comfortable playing the role of Dad in my family. Then, this past winter, my own father showed up with that MySpace message. After I read it, I looked at his profile to see what I'd been missing.

His whole page was dedicated to a TV show he hosts in Maryland, where he interviews rap stars like M.O.P., Sheek Louch, Ja Rule, and Chris Brown. I had no idea he was doing all of this. I saw a lot of pictures of him with various rappers. Even though I was angry, I have to admit, I was also impressed. I'm a big fan of hip-hop, and for him to know these rappers personally made me eager to learn more.

I typed a message to him filled with questions like, "Where have you been all this time?" and, "Why are you contacting me now?" and, "How has your life been?" Even though I was angry with him, I still wanted to know what his life was like.

Before I clicked "Send," I thought about it for an eternity. Should I send it and open myself up to being shot down again, or should I give him the same cold shoulder he'd given me all my life? Eventually I gave in because I really wanted to speak with him. I was overcome with curiosity.

He was online so he messaged me right back, and we began messaging back and forth. With every message I received, my heart beat a little faster. My father sending me messages was a small gesture, but to me it showed he was becoming consistent for the first time in my life—every time I messaged him, he answered right back.

In the end we got a lot of our feelings out in the open. He told me that he felt bad for not being there for my childhood, and that he'd take it back if he could. I told him that my life was hard and that I needed him here with me. He wrote, "I'm really sorry." By the time I signed off that night, I was feeling pretty good about our relationship.

But it wasn't long before my father was up to his old tricks. A couple of days after we began messaging, he asked me to meet up with him in Manhattan. He comes to New York once a month to do interviews for his TV show. He asked me if I wanted to come to an interview in Manhattan and watch him work. I agreed because I hadn't seen him in so long and the thought of meeting rappers made me want to believe him.

Up until the day before the interview, he messaged me regularly to remind me to be there. The night before, I couldn't sleep. It felt like Christmas Eve. When morning came, I was anxious. I got dressed and was ready to go by noon like he had told me. I waited for his phone call until about 3 p.m., when I fell asleep on my bed.

When I woke up it was about 7 p.m. and all I could think was that I had missed his call. I went to the phone and saw that there were no missed calls from him. I just went back to sleep and I didn't talk to anybody for the rest of the night. I felt so gullible for believing him. I knew it was his fault for lying to me again, but I couldn't help feeling like it was also my fault for trusting him.

MySpace tells you if the person you're messaging is currently online. A couple of days after my father stood me up, I noticed that he was online. Rather than send him a message, I waited for him to do it because I felt it was up to him to tell me what had happened.

When he didn't, I thought that he just didn't care enough to tell me why he couldn't call me. Eventually I gave up and signed off. After that, I decided I was through. He'd done this too many times before. We haven't spoken or written to each other since. Only time will tell if we end up contacting each other again, but for now, I doubt it.

Soon after that, my father told my half brother (his other son) to tell me that we can't meet up until the summer because he's too into his music. There was no apology and he didn't even acknowledge that he'd stood me up. It was pathetic. He couldn't even talk to me like a man. It was the kind of cowardliness I've learned to expect from my "father."

I'll always be curious about what could've been and whether my life would be any different if my father had stayed around. But I'm realizing now that I don't think he would have measured up to what I was searching for in a father figure.

As I see it, my father is far from a man. A man takes care of his responsibilities. A man owns up to his mistakes and tries his best to correct them. A man doesn't give up on raising a child before he even starts. I've been raised by real men like my neighbor John. And with John's help, I'm learning to be one myself.

I'm proud of myself because I went out and found who I needed in my life all by myself, and I'm doing everything I can to become the man my father never was. I've helped raise my younger brother and I plan on continuing to give him the educational and emotional support that he wants and needs, whenever he needs it.

That's what a man does.

Rashad was 16 when he wrote this story.

Rafael Manashirov

Camp Rising Sun: Where Guys Can Be Guys

By Jamal Greene

For eight weeks one summer, I was secluded with 55 other young guys. There were only five times when we saw girls. Very few of us saw our families. And you know what?

I enjoyed it.

Before you jump to any conclusions, I'm neither homosexual nor antisocial and I didn't spend last summer on Parris Island or at some other military training base. I spent the summer about two hours north of New York City, at Camp Rising Sun in a town called Red Hook.

If you were to look in the camp's brochure, you would probably see something about teaching motivated youngsters the meaning of cooperation and brotherhood and responsibility, or something like that. And then you would probably say to yourself, "I don't want to join the Marines." Well, Camp Rising Sun isn't the Marines. You'll meet more foreigners at Rising Sun and have more contact with females than in the Marines.

But I didn't go because I was trying to meet more foreigners or because I wanted to get away from women. I went because I didn't have anything better to do and I thought it might be fun. (A social studies teacher suggested it, and since the camp doesn't charge, I knew I could afford it.)

As I was lugging my overpacked suitcase up to "tent hill" on the first day of camp, I met Jed Wood, one of my four tent mates. He was also lugging a suitcase up the hill, and having almost as much trouble as I was. I looked him over and quickly concluded that he was from New Jersey, not taking into account the warped Southern twang in his accent. Don't ask me why, but he just had that "Jersey air" about him.

"Where you from?" I asked, only as a formality.

"Provo, Utah," he responded with a smile.

Utah? But he wasn't wearing black argyle socks up to his knees! He wasn't amazed by electricity and running water and all the other modern conveniences that we civilized New Yorkers take for granted! He even spoke English! How could he possibly be from Utah?

I would later find out that Jed was also a Mormon, which was my second surprise. I knew Mormons were the people who sponsored those weird commercials that said "Church of Jesus Christ of Latter Day Saints," at the end. I thought their only purpose in life was to put out those commercials.

Jed was different. He frequently spoke of his multiple girl-friends, his love of fly-fishing, and his bug collection. OK, so maybe he wasn't exactly like me, but he did have a personality.

When we reached Buck Palace, which was our tent's name, we encountered another tent mate. His name was Ola (pro-nounced Ula) Holst Vea, and he was a blond, blue-eyed kid from Norway. Ola had a beaming smile on his face and, as I would learn over the course of the summer, he was very rarely unhappy about anything.

The very first day in the tent, Ola was sticking his face out through the tent flaps and shouting various harsh words at people. It wasn't that he was angry at anybody. He was just showing off his knowledge of American curses. Cursing, by the way, is strictly forbidden in Mormon doctrine, so Jed was not a happy camper when he first heard Ola's ranting.

That first week of camp, Jed and Ola were both assigned to "mess" squad, which meant that they had to wash dishes after all the meals (which every camper must do at some point). If you've ever washed massive amounts of dishes side by side with another person, you know that when you're finished you're either the best of friends or the worst of enemies. Jed and Ola were almost inseparable after a week, so I guess they fell into the first category.

The first time we met the girls, the bathroom was teeming with guys getting haircuts.

I learned a bit more about Ola on our canoe trip. Every camper at Rising Sun goes on either a hiking trip or a canoe trip, depending on which you like more and on how well you can swim. During the third week of camp, Ola and I could be found in a two-man canoe floating down a lazy river in the Adirondack Mountains.

It was in this canoe that I learned that Ola was something of a political revolutionary in Norway and that his goal in life was to rid the world of rich capitalists through non-violent means. It amazed me that I, a kid from Brooklyn, was spending part of my summer canoeing through the Adirondacks with some strange Norwegian hybrid of Karl Marx and Mahatma Gandhi.

While Ola was easily the most colorful member of Buck Palace, he was not the only interesting character. Although most of the things we did at camp were led by campers, every tent had to have an adult counselor. Our counselor was a college theater major from Minnesota named Jon Liseth. Jon wore glasses and lots of pastel-colored shirts, so at first I figured he was a real herb. But my first night in the tent, I found myself chuckling at Jon's "Minnesota humor."

There was one other person in my tent. His name was Ahmed Mahmood and he was from Brooklyn, just like me. Since he was from Brooklyn, I figured we would get along right off the bat. While we did get along OK, I was probably closer to the Mormon and Norwegian by the end of the summer than I was to my fellow Brooklynite.

D uring the first assembly, we had to sit with our tent mates. Every day, a different camper acted as leader, or "sachem." The sachem set the day's schedule and led the roll call at assemblies. When the sachem called "Buck Palace," I felt a strange pride. Our tent housed five different religions, three different races, two different countries, and four different states. But for the two weeks that I was in that tent (all campers change tents every two weeks), we were not Ahmed, Jed, Ola, Jon, and Jamal. We were just "Buck Palace."

OK, so maybe it sounds a little like Soviet Russia or the Borg from Star Trek, but it isn't. Individuality is welcome, even encouraged, at Camp Rising Sun. If you want to walk around wearing nothing but Bermuda shorts and knee-high tube socks, it doesn't matter. You are among friends.

Part of the reason may be because we were an all-boys camp. It's amazing how truly difficult it is to be oneself in New York City's social setting, when we are constantly surrounded by the opposite sex. Guys try to ooze machismo when they are around girls. They become a persona, an entirely different person than their true selves.

Case in point: Camp Rising Sun is divided into a boys camp in Red Hook and a girls camp 10 miles away in Clinton Corners. The two camps meet each other five times during the summer.

The first time we met the girls, the bathroom was teeming with guys getting haircuts, taking 45-minute showers, and wiping the dust off their hair gel and Q-tips at 4:30 in the morning. These were some of the same guys who had not showered in a week and a half, had been wearing the same underwear for three days, and had gotten up five minutes after the breakfast bell the morning before.

So, I guess I learned a few lessons about human nature from Camp Rising Sun. I now know that females are not the only ones who obsess over their appearance. But more seriously, I learned something that I thought I knew but really didn't. There are no innate differences between people. If we are placed in an environment in which we can be ourselves without fear of alienation, we are all the same at heart.

Jamal was 17 when he wrote this story. He attended Harvard University and Yale Law School, and became an associate professor at Columbia Law School.

Matty DeLuna

Getting Ghetto

By Fred Wagenhauser

Would you be interested to hear another Eminem story about a white kid who's been through so much? White kids trying to be ghetto—it sounds like an "Animorph" book, but it's a reality. I'm white, I live in the projects, I can rap and all my life I've made friends with danger and deceit.

My roots in "urban culture" started while I was just a kid living in New Jersey with my Aunt Trish and Uncle Lenny. That side of the family was mixed and threw me into a world of hip-hop and r&b.

I liked rap from the jump. I could vibe the lyrics about how hard it was living in the streets because my family had to scrounge to make ends meet. As for r&b, I loved the way Donell Jones' "Where I Wanna Be" and Musiq Soulchild's "Don't Change" sang about love and loss.

Now, my family has never been stereotypically white. By that I mean acting like you got a bad smell under your nose, have never been arrested, have a lot of money and stay away from the projects. My family is not like that. We don't have money, we're not snobs and some of us have been in foster care or locked up.

My brother bangs with the six (rolls with a crew) and he's always in trouble. My mother was in foster care when she was little, and when people meet her they know she's real. One time when I riding in the car with my mom, I put on Power 105 and a Snoop Dogg throwback came on.

My mother said, "Oh, this is my @#$%!" and she started to sing along with Snoop and Dre. She's gangsta.

When I was 9 we moved from Jersey to Brentwood, on Long Island, where my mom grew up. When I got to the block, all I heard playing was reggae, Spanish music and of course blazin' hip-hop and r&b. Jersey had been peaceful and quiet, but Brentwood was noisy and crowded and chaotic. I loved it.

When September came, 3rd grade was cool and fun but there was one problem: I was a nerd, from how I talked to how I dressed. My family never really had money like that, so I was in Payless kicks and some Wal-Mart clothes. I was always made fun of.

The next year my mom said I was going to a new school. I was happy. Maybe it would be a new start for me. But again, the same things: I had no gear and I was a nerd. What friends I did make wanted me to change.

"Fred, why do you wear such tight pants?" Harry asked one day.

"My mother doesn't have it like that," I told him. I felt embarrassed and annoyed, because it's nobody's business why I dress the way I do. But eventually it started to eat at me on the inside.

I asked my mother if I could get new jeans so I wouldn't get picked on. The next time my family took me shopping, I picked out the baggy jeans instead of the nut huggers. I was so happy because I got more respect.

Then the tables turned. One day at lunch when I was 11 years old, my friends (who were all black and Latino, like most of the kids in my school) told me I was a "wigger." I didn't know what that word meant until Harry told me it was a white person trying to be black.

That's when I realized that some of the things I did to fit in are not just stereotypically black, but stereotypically ghetto.

Then, when I was 13 years old, I beat up a kid in my middle school and was sent to a residential treatment center, St. Mary's. In that environment,

I felt that because I was white I had to be the toughest and meanest kid on the wing to get respect.

everyone assumed that since I was white and smart I was a nerd. But when they heard my poetry about my life struggles, it wiped the smirk off their faces.

Then I got sent to a lockdown upstate. I don't like to fight but I will if I have to. So I was fighting a lot just to prove to everyone I wasn't an ass. I felt that because I was white I had to be the toughest and meanest kid on the wing to get respect. I had to learn how to freestyle and battle rap and keep up on the new slang coming in. All this just so I could watch TV in peace.

One time, the whole wing was bored so a few kids started to battle rap. James said, "Come on, Fred, it's just like poetry." I tried and messed up but it was cool so I practiced. I started to speak what was on my mind in front of people.

Those experiences taught me to use my voice. I've always been a really shy person. I'm not good in crowds. In general, I really don't believe in myself. When I found out I could survive in lockdown and that I had a little flow, my confidence rose.

But now that I'm right on the borderline of adulthood, I feel I need to change certain aspects of my ghetto ways. I have to calm down a lot. I get into fights on the regular and in the past six months I've been to the bookings three times. Plus, I don't have a real job, I'm not in school and I'm on the verge of homelessness. It's real hard.

Sometimes I feel it in my bones that if I don't get out of my neighborhood soon, someone's going to get hurt. I don't want to do that. I want to expand my mind. Learning about hip hop style and music, and to fight, deal and battle rap—those are not the only things I want to learn in life.

I'm hoping to take my ass to college far away from the Lowa Deck (my 'hood, the Lower East Side). But I wonder if I can go to school far from here, and if I do, am I really going to calm down on the criminal stuff? I'm not gonna sit here, lie and say "I'm gonna change" when I don't know if I will.

Now that I'm on the borderline of adulthood, I feel I need to change certain aspects of my ghetto ways.

I want the best of both worlds in the palm of my hand. I want to be able to do my thing on job interviews and amaze college professors with my vast intellect, and on the flip side, walk through the projects because I know mad people from different walks of life.

I want to show people color doesn't define me. I want to bring my hunger and the ability to adapt that I got from the streets and apply it to making a straight life. That's my uniqueness. But dealing and getting locked up? Nah. I have to be able to control my anger and get out the damn ghetto.

I fear losing my voice and my confidence. I also fear I might get in too deep and bang, I'm caught up again. But I hope that understanding the dangers that living crooked has in store for me will help me find a new way to stand up and be me.

Fred was 21 when he wrote this story.

Stephanie "Meadow" Kunar

Am I the Father?

By Anonymous

One day in June, I received a phone call from a female acquaintance. We were talking normally until she came out of nowhere and said, "I'm pregnant and I think it's yours." My eyes opened wide, and I asked her when this happened. "Remember back on October 2?" she said. "We did something."

I was stunned as I remembered what she was talking about. Then I couldn't think too well because anger came over me. I asked in a loud tone of voice, "How long did you know this? How many months are you?"

She told me that the baby was due next week and I was the father. I was furious. She had known this for nine months and was telling me only a week before the baby was due. I hung up on her.

I sat there trying to get my thoughts together. I knew the time she was talking about. Back in October I was chilling and getting drunk at a party and I saw her across the room. I approached her and asked how she was doing. She said, "I've been eyeing you all night, and was waiting for you to come to me."

I was amazed. I thought, "Oh really? Damn. This means I don't have to do that much." We went upstairs where the music wasn't so loud so we could talk alone. She told me that her name was Melanie and that she didn't have a man but was looking for one.

I said I was looking for someone, too. That was a lie. Really, I did have a woman, but I figured what Melanie didn't know wouldn't hurt her.

Melanie started telling me about her life. She said her moms was a pain in the behind. She had an older brother who didn't care too much about her. I was kinda interested in her little tale. She said, "Let me get your number and we can talk on the phone sometime." I saw nothing wrong with that. She was cool enough and cute.

Then next thing I knew Melanie started to fall asleep next to me. I tried to wake her up, and she pulled me towards her. We stared in each other's eyes for a hot second, and before I knew it she was kissing my cheek. So me being drunk, and she being drunk, we did our thang.

I felt weird after we had sex. I hadn't had a one-night stand before. I felt I straight up took advantage of her, and that seemed strange. After we were done, I left her and we never spoke again. But we kept hearing about each other through mutual friends. I just thought of her as a female I met at a party.

But now she had called me, nine months later, telling me a baby had come out of that night and that it would be in the world in a week. I felt very confused and I wanted to punch something.

Instead, I called my girl, who I had only recently started seeing, and told her what was going down. My lady sounded stunned on the phone but helped me think through the situation.

We both thought that the first thing I needed to do was to take a paternity test to see if the kid was really mine. We weren't ready yet to think too far beyond that. I kept asking myself, "What if it is mine? Am I ready to be a father? Am I ready to take care of another life?"

If it was mine, I wasn't going to abandon it. I've seen too many fathers leave their kids behind. In fact, my own father left me behind when he went to jail.

I knew the pain of growing up without a dad, and I always swore I wouldn't do that if I had a child. So I knew if I became a father, my teenage life was gone.

She told me that the baby was due next week and I was the father.

I would have to stop acting like a boy and take care of my responsibilities as a man.

I didn't know what that meant, exactly. I didn't know whether it meant I would have to quit school to get a full-time job. I did know I was too young for this. What's worse, I didn't have a penny to my name. But the baby would need things—diapers, a crib, toys, clothes, milk.

So many thoughts in my head, so many things to do, and the way I saw it was that I didn't have much time to do those things. The walls were closing quick and I felt I had no one to help me.

I couldn't go back to selling drugs on the street. What good would I be to my kid if I were dead or locked up? I couldn't go to my parents—they would kill me. How the hell could I tell my moms that I had a kid? How could I tell any of my family members?

I felt ashamed. I was supposed to be the one who succeeded, who didn't get caught in situations like this.

The only thing I knew was that I wanted to stay with my girl and I wanted to be part of this kid's life. No matter what the circumstances were, I wasn't leaving my seed. But how was I ever going to handle getting along with the kid's mother, someone who would be there in the kid's life forever, someone I couldn't stand for putting me through this?

Melanie called me back and asked why I hung up on her. I told her, "You knew all this and held out on me for this long, and you wondering why I am being mean to you? I want nothing to do with you. I want to be with my lady and that's it. The only reason I am going be nice to you and show some respect towards you is for the kid."

I knew I was half responsible for all this and that made me even madder. I wanted to hit someone, anyone. I wanted to slap her through the damn phone. But I don't hit females.

At the time it was around graduation, and I had to pass the tests I needed to graduate. As I was studying for the tests and, later, taking them, my mind was on the baby. I could think of nothing but the baby, my girl, my family, and how was I gonna make money.

For a while I thought that my girl would leave, too, for the simple fact that females hate dealing with baby mama drama. Still, she continued to stand by me.

"Why would I leave?" she said when I told her what I was afraid of. "I said I was going to be there for you and that's what I'm doing."

My friends who I told about the baby situation were shocked about the news, but they supported me 100%. I couldn't ask for better friends in a time of need.

But that didn't mean everything was good. I was nervous just thinking about becoming a father, and even with the best friends and girl in the world, I wasn't ready.

I had an idea how hard it is to be a good parent. After all, neither of my parents pulled it off well enough to keep me at home, and so I ended up in foster care. It hurt that my father had always been in and out of my life.

So when I'd thought of having kids myself, I wanted everything to be perfect. I wanted to have two seeds, a boy and a girl, or as I would call them, my prince and princess. I pictured having my seeds by the wife I chose to marry and that I would be financially stable enough to take care of them. Not to have everything completely opposite—to have a kid by someone who I don't care for, and to raise a kid when I'm not stable.

On a Thursday in June, Melanie had the baby. She called me two hours after she delivered and told me that it was a boy. I was happy to hear that it had gone well with her and that the baby was healthy.

I went to the hospital that Friday to take the paternity test. As the doctor took some blood for my DNA, he said the results wouldn't be ready for a few days. I felt weird having the blood drawn. My arm was flinching as he did it. I couldn't stop thinking about how all of this was happening so fast.

Afterward I went to see the baby. He was sleeping and beautiful. The last time I saw a

I knew the pain of growing up without a dad.

baby that beautiful was when my lil' sister was born. I asked the nurse if I could hold him, and she gave me the baby.

I sat there holding Shorty in my arms like a prized possession. I started talking to the baby like I already knew it was mine. He was cute, with hazel eyes, a little hair, and little hands and feet.

When the nurse told me that she had to put him back in the crib, I didn't want to let him go. The whole feeling that the baby was mine hit me hard. I saw Shorty's eyes and I knew that I would be ready for this. He was my responsibility and I wouldn't let him down.

The whole time I was in the hospital room, Melanie and I didn't communicate. The only time we spoke was when it regarded the baby. I told Melanie, "My only plans are to raise that baby, nothing else." She said she understood that.

I told her I would get the diapers and some toys, though I still hadn't figured out how. She said she and her mother would supply the clothes and the crib and I could see the kid whenever

I wanted.

I said I'd see Shorty after school and some nights that I had free. Melanie's moms was in the hospital, too. She seemed to like me, but she was also mad at me because she knew that we were too young and that we weren't ready for this.

Monday was the big day—the day I'd find out if the kid was really mine. At the end of the day, I was supposed to meet my lady and tell her the results.

When I got to the hospital I saw Shorty moving, and I asked the doctor if I could hold him while he went and got the results. So I sat there in a chair holding Shorty in my arms, rocking back and forth.

I started talking to him, telling him, "Hey, little one, I might be your father," and, "Don't worry, I will never leave you." I knew I was getting a little too mushy with Shorty, but I couldn't help it. I even felt the urge to cry and let some feelings out.

The way the baby moved in my arms was a joyous feeling to me. He was lying there sleeping, eyes closed, his little fists tight. I couldn't believe this was mine.

I started talking to the baby like I already knew it was mine.

After a while, Melanie caught my attention. She was just outside the room and I saw that she was crying. Her mother got up and started yelling at the doctor, "It has to be him." I walked toward them, and as the yelling got louder, the baby started crying and the nurse took him away.

Melanie's mother told the doctor, "I'll pay you to tell him he is the father." I couldn't believe what I was hearing. Then I felt like I was about to flip out on her.

As I struggled to stay calm, the doctor pulled me to the side and told me eye-to-eye, face-to-face, that the child wasn't mine. I felt strange—both sad and overjoyed. I knew I wasn't ready to be a father, but I had been liking the idea of having a kid to call mine.

That night, I told my girl the news. She was glad. But later as I walked down the streets, I noticed all the babies who were with their fathers and I started to miss Shorty. It was strange, all I'd been through in the last week because of that one-night mistake with Melanie. It was stranger to think that I could've been a father.

I call Melanie up once in a while to check up on Shorty. See how he's holding up. I was mad at her for doing all that to me, but I came out all right and she is having to give up her teen years.

To be honest, I believe some good has come out of it for me. My lady and I are stronger as a couple after going through that together, and I'm much more cautious about sex. Let's just say I always use a condom. I know that having kids isn't my thing, not now. (Maybe when I'm about 22 and financially stable, I'll think about it.)

After seeing Shorty and holding him in my arms, I see the love fathers have for their kids. But I also see why so many run. It's frightening to look at something so small and know how much it needs you. But that don't make it right for fathers to leave.

The writer was 19 when he wrote this story.
He attended LaGuardia Community College.

Teo Romero

Getting Back My Heart

By Daniel Verzhbo

"Why do you keep doing this to yourself?" my mother asked me with a tear rolling down her cheek. Lots of thoughts were running through my head, but I couldn't find the words to answer her question. I had just gotten arrested for shoplifting, and I was ashamed of myself.

For the past year and a half I'd been messing up my life, but I didn't realize it. Hanging out with my friends and smoking weed was like living a dream for me. I didn't have to worry about anything. Every time I got high, all my stress went away.

Back then I was too stupid to realize that my friends were only there when I had money in my pocket. And I didn't notice that what I was doing was pulling my mother and me apart. I wasn't listening to her at all, and I'd rarely be home to help her.

When my mom picked me up from the police precinct I felt

like there was no future for me. It's hard to admit, but I was depressed.

I didn't know what to expect from my mother, but she didn't give me any punishments. "This is the last chance that I'm going to give you," she said.

For the next couple of weeks I tried to stay away from negativity, but the craving for weed kept pulling me back to my friends like a magnet. And that's when my friends had this crazy idea of running away. At first I was like, "Hell no," but after a couple of blunts I didn't care.

We went to Times Square in Manhattan and spent a couple of days there, but after a while I was broke and tired so I decided to go home. It was around 5:30 in the morning and I was about to get on the train, when a couple of police officers stopped me and asked me for ID.

After asking me more questions, they said that I had to come with them. And that's when I got really nervous. Did they have a warrant for my arrest? Did my mom report me missing? What was going on?

"I'm just going to check on you and call your parents," the cop told me. "Now sit down and be quiet."

When he finally reached my mother, I felt relieved that I had someone on my side to pick me up.

I started to hang out with the wrong people, but I never thought it would go this far.

During their conversation I remember the cop telling my mother, "Miss, do you know that this is child neglect?" I had no idea what that meant. But then the police officer made a couple more phone calls and drove me to a strange-looking building. Some lady there started asking me tons of questions, like if my mother ever abused me and if I ever felt suicidal.

I asked the woman what was going to happen to me next. She said that I was going to a foster home.

"Why?" I asked her, with pain in my heart.

"Because," she said slowly, not trying to hurt my feelings, "your mother doesn't want you anymore."

As soon as those words got through my brain I thought it was the end of the world. I couldn't believe it! My heart froze, and broke in a thousand little pieces.

That night I was in a group home with a whole bunch of questions, like, "What is wrong with my mother? Why would she leave me like that? Does she still love me?" I felt like I was lost on an island with no map.

A couple days later I was on my way to a foster home. I was really shy at first, and didn't want to talk to anyone about myself. Most of the time I stayed in my room, and just thought about all the wonderful times that my mother and I had spent together.

I wondered how she felt saying those words to put me in foster care, the words that affected me so much.

When I was growing up, my mother and I were always close. My childhood in Russia was peaceful and I had lots of family around to support me. Even on bad days, being with my mom made my day turn good. I felt like she was always there whenever I needed her. And I knew that nothing would ever happen to me while I was in her arms.

But when we moved to America we were on our own, and that was hard on both of us. My mother was struggling and had to work very hard for only a few dollars. I didn't have anyone to talk to, and no big family there to love me. My mother gave me lots of love, but when she left me I was always bored and lonely.

I guess that's what pulled us away from each other. She had to work and leave me at times, and I needed someone to be with while she was not there. I started to hang out with the wrong people and not listen to her. But I never thought it would go this far.

I wanted to apologize to my mom for causing her all this stress. I never thought of how much it hurt her. She created me and then couldn't take care of me, so that's double the pain for her. At that point I didn't know who was the failure—me, or my mother.

I felt really guilty about what I'd done and really worried about my relationship with my mother, so after a couple of days I decided to call her.

"Mom, I miss you, and I'm sorry," were the first words that came out of my mouth, and with them came tears.

"I don't know what to tell you," she said with disappointment. At that point I felt like this conversation was going to be a dead end.

"I love you, and really want to see you again," I said.

"Why did you run away?" she asked.

"I don't know," I said, trying to avoid answering.

"Well, think about it."

"I was really bored staying home all the time, and I wanted to hang out with my friends…"

"Don't you realize that these friends of yours are leading your life to nowhere?" she asked me, blowing her nose. "Matter of fact, even worse than nowhere—to jail, and to growing up to be a nobody. Is that what you want to be, a nobody?"

"Of course not," I quickly answered.

I promised my mom that I would be a "new me" and try to succeed in life. Then I asked her the biggest question on my mind: "Why don't you want me anymore?"

After a long pause and a sigh she finally answered me. "You need a break, a break where you look at yourself and your behavior," she said. "For now I feel like I can't help you anymore. I have been trying, and my way was not working."

I begged my mom for one more chance, but she said that she'd given me plenty and I'd messed up every one.

"Daniel, I love you with all my heart, and this is as hard for me as it is for you," she said. "But I think that this option will be best for you for now. You could have gotten locked up or even hurt. I don't want that to happen. I want you to be something in life."

I promised my mom I would try my best.

Then we talked about ways I could change my behavior. She said that the faster I improved my behavior, the faster I'd be home. When I hung up the phone I felt much better. I knew now that my mom still cared about me. Before this phone call I thought that she wasn't ever going to speak to me again.

Even though I felt hurt by her decision, it helped me to get a hold of myself and get back on track. I was determined to show my mother that I wasn't a failure. I felt I had the strength to improve myself, not only to get my mother back, but also to get back my positive self. I felt like it was going to be a long process, but I was ready for it.

*I*t was really hard to live without my mother in my life. I could only see her twice a week, and that wasn't enough.

When we would see each other at my social worker's office we would talk for hours about random things, and afterwards she would take me out to eat somewhere. The first couple of times I felt strange seeing my mother, because she and I were like two different people now.

It didn't seem normal getting to know someone all over again when you'd known the person for your whole life. But I could feel that this was the best thing that I was doing for myself. Even though it was a little weird, it felt like I was getting back my heart.

Visit by visit, our relationship improved. But at times I still felt like a stranger. Sometimes we would have bad days, and with bad days came arguments. I hated arguing with the only person in America who loved me. But I couldn't control my mouth and my anger.

I expected my mom to be less hard on me after I left her, but she was much stricter than before. I didn't know that learning to listen to my mother would be so hard.

Sometimes I would get angry because my mom was trying to gain control over me, and I felt that she had lost the right to control me when she put me in foster care. Sometimes the thought of her leaving me again would come to my mind, and that would make me the angriest of all.

I didn't want to ask my mom if she would put me in care again because I was shy, and because I really didn't want to hear her answer. Instead, I'd get angry and start arguments for no reason.

I knew that my anger was one of the things that I needed to improve if I wanted to go home. And I definitely wanted to go home. I felt that if I could live with my mother, we could have a good future together.

So after a while I learned to overcome that fear of going back into care by telling myself that my mother would never do that to me. I also told myself that if I behaved well and listened to her, the thought wouldn't ever occur to her. I started to feel her love again, and that gave me more confidence.

The more my mother and I saw each other and talked to each other, the stronger our relationship grew. During our visits, my mother was only focused on me. I loved that feeling of knowing that someone actually cared about me. It felt good. It felt like I had someone on my side to be there for me.

I was determined to show my mother that I wasn't a failure.

In a few weeks I'll be getting discharged and will go home to my mother. I'm not going to mess our relationship up for anything. If my mom gets a job and can't spend lots of time with me, I'll be ready for it. I've found some new friends who are more positive, and I know what could happen if I go back to the past.

I'm not the only one who has been trying to improve to make our relationship stronger. My mother is going to parenting classes and is trying to be the best mother that she can.

Even though we still have arguments once in a blue, we resolve them with a peaceful talk instead of screaming at each other for hours. I feel that my mother and I are a strong team now, ready for anything.

Knowing that I'm going to live with my mother again is the best feeling that I've ever experienced. The future ahead of us gives us a chance to build a new relationship, one that I strongly hope will last forever.

Daniel was 16 when he wrote this story.

YC Art Dept.

Becoming a Man, Jewish Style

By Chris Kanarick

If I had a nickel for every time one of my friends told me that I was lucky to be Jewish because I got to have a bar mitzvah, I'd probably be buying out Donald Trump by now. When they think of a bar mitzvah, a lot of people imagine a wild party, lots of money, and expensive gifts. But a bar mitzvah means a lot more to a Jewish person than that.

When a Jewish boy reaches the age of 13, he becomes a bar mitzvah or "son of the commandments." The ceremony takes place in the temple. The boy stands at the *bima* (podium), recites something called a *Haftorah*, and reads a portion from the *Torah* (that's what we call the first five books of the Bible). Both are written in Hebrew, so you have to study and practice to do it.

At the end, he makes a speech and thanks his parents and the rabbi for helping him through the whole thing. Once a boy is bar mitzvahed, he becomes a man in the eyes of the Jewish religion.

After the ceremony, there is a large party. All the relatives come, and the band plays the Jewish hits, like Hava Nagila. Everybody dances, eats, and has a good time.

Now, my bar mitzvah didn't exactly go as planned. You see, mom had been looking forward to this for a long time, and she was planning to throw me a big gala affair, even though we couldn't afford it.

So, I practiced for months with the rabbi. It was not as easy as I thought. I had to learn how to pronounce the Hebrew words correctly and then I had to learn how to chant them correctly. It wasn't enough that I could say the prayer. I had to chant it, like now I'm the Indian chief or something. But I did it, I got through the whole thing. I kept practicing and practicing. I felt like Rocky, like I was warming up for a fight with the big bad prayer book.

Finally, the big day came. I don't think I need to tell you I was pretty nervous. I just knew I was going to screw up. I was never good at public speaking. That's why I never ran for class president—I didn't want to give a campaign speech.

I stood up there on the *bima*. I looked out at the proud, smiling faces of my friends and family, people who I knew cared enough to come watch me in all my glory. I recognized my mother in the front row with my grandparents and all my relatives who had come from all over to see me. It was pretty deep.

I looked at my book, chanted the first word, and dropped my head dead on the desk in front of me. Of course, many people got worried at the sight of this and gasps arose from the audience. The rabbi, realizing that there was a problem, quickly rose from his chair and came over to me. He tried to calm me down, to no avail.

As I stood there looking like a fool, a little boy that I didn't even know came up from the audience and tapped me. When I looked down at him, he told me not to worry and that I would be fine.

After a few minutes of childish sobbing (just kidding, wanted to see if you were paying attention), the rabbi turned the little desk that the book was resting on towards the side and I continued facing sideways until I felt comfortable. I eventually reached the end and...I was a man.

A man who had just embarrassed himself in front of friends and family, but a man nonetheless.

All the time I was preparing for my entrance into manhood, my mother had been busy planning the reception. The party not only had to be big and terribly expensive, it also had to be color-coordinated. The balloons had to match the tablecloths, the tablecloths had to match the napkins, the napkins had to match the plates, and I had to match everything in the room, including the rest of my family. We all wore blue and gray.

I was looking forward to the party. Mom was determined to make this the biggest one since the Boston Tea Party. When the limo arrived (see what I mean) we hopped in and were off. The party was at this big banquet hall-type place called Colonial Mansions.

When we walked in, the room was filled with blue and gray balloons. I thought this was the room where the party would be held. It wasn't. The actual party room was even bigger and more lavishly decorated. There were a lot of tables with a big balloon centerpiece on each one. The table where the kids sat (pretty hypocritical right? I just became

I was pretty nervous. I just knew I was going to screw up.

a man and I still had to sit at the kids' table) had a big balloon arch over it.

There was a live band in the corner and a big empty space in the middle for dancing (which, by the way, I don't do).

First, the band played a really cheesy song, "We Are Family," and introduced my family and me. Next, I went to stand by the big cake and waited while Grandpa Max cut the *challah* (a braided loaf of bread made with eggs).

Next, we did the candle-lighting ceremony, where I called up those people who are special to me (actually to mom because she made up the list), like my grandparents and aunts and uncles, and they lit candles. Then my immediate family—mother, stepfather, sisters, and brother—came up. I made a wish and blew out the candles.

I just became a man and I still had to sit at the kids' table.

After that, we all gathered around in a circle. We did the old dance called the *hora*. This is where everyone holds hands and moves around in a circle to traditional Jewish songs. Then, a few of the guys, like my stepfather and his friends, got me into a chair. They lifted it up in the air with me in it and spun me around, while these people who allegedly cared about me watched.

There I was, high up off the ground, and I just knew one of these guys was going to have to sneeze. Luckily, I landed safely and the rest of the family got in the death seat (one at a time, of course).

After a little more dancing, we sat down to eat. After that, everyone (except me) went back to dancing.

A bar mitzvah is great because it's a chance for the whole family to get together on a happy occasion. I saw relatives I hadn't seen in a long time. I saw relatives I'd never even met. Half the people there I didn't know! My mom would walk over and ask, "Did you say hello to Aunt Jean?"

"Huh?" I'd reply. I had a lot more relatives than I thought.

We partied until everybody went home and then we went home. Despite the fact that a lot of weird stuff happened and that I spent most of the night telling the guy who was videotaping the party to back off, I had a good time.

One of the things they ask you to write about in your speech is what this day means to you. Well, to me it meant that I was to have more responsibility in the Jewish community. As a bar mitzvah, I was now allowed to hold the Torah. I could be honored by being called up to open the Ark where the Torah is kept. I was considered an actual part of the congregation.

For those of you out there who are reaching the age of your bar mitzvah, just do your best. Your parents will be proud whether you breeze through the whole thing like an expert or you make a floundering idiot of yourself like I did. Also, remember that a bar mitzvah is more than a way to make fast money. It's a privilege and an honor.

And, okay, the money's pretty cool, too.

Chris was 17 when he wrote this story.

Fernando Garcia

A Girl Takes Control

By Troy Shawn Welcome

I was walking down the street with my best friend a couple of months ago when he slipped on a mountain of snow and almost fell down. I started laughing, he started laughing, and a group of girls from across the street started laughing.

We kept walking, but one of the girls called out, "You, in the all black, come here." We couldn't see what they looked like because the street corner they were standing on was very dark. After thinking it over, we decided to go and see.

"You look mad good," a husky, dark-skinned female blurted out. She reminded me of the wrestler Sergeant Slaughter.

"Damn, this girl looks rough," I was thinking. She wasn't even cute. I was speechless.

"Word?" I said.

One of her friends, a short-haired, dark-skinned girl said,

"I'm sayin', she was watching you from when you was down the block, so I think ya'll should just say ya'll words."

I was double shocked. I couldn't believe that I was actually having to take in the words that I was used to dishing out. And it didn't stop there.

"You got a girl?" Sgt. Slaughter anxiously asked.

"Not really," I said.

"You got a commitment?" she countered.

I told her that I didn't, but for the life of me, I don't know why. Probably because I love to flirt.

Then she asked for my number, but neither one of us had a pen. Unfortunately, one of her friends did. I didn't feel like dissing her, so when she asked again, I gave her a number. It wasn't mine, but I'm sure it was somebody's.

There were a couple of reasons why I gave her a wrong number. First of all, she wasn't my type at all. I mean, she looked like she could kick King Kong's butt. The other thing that bothered me was how she talked to me.

It was a weird feeling to be talked to in the same way that I sometimes talk to females. I was intimidated by the way she spoke to me. I'm accustomed to being in control when I'm try-

I'm accustomed to being in control when I'm trying to talk to a girl.

ing to talk to a girl or when she's trying to talk to me, but this girl was dropping line after line on me. I didn't have enough time to think. I didn't like that feeling at all.

You see, we guys love to be in control. It's our nature to plan on how we're going to get a female and imagine we're the ones making all the decisions. We don't realize that women know what they're doing too. But even if that's true, girls usually let us go on thinking we're the ones in control.

Sgt. Slaughter didn't bother to do that. She just came right out and told me what she wanted.

As unpleasant and dominating as she was, being stopped by her boosted my ego. The experience made me feel mad good about myself, like I was the man, like I was mad phat.

A female, on the other hand, probably wouldn't think of it in that way. Females are always getting approached in the streets and probably get tired of it. She gets so many comments a day that she probably thinks more about her safety than her ego.

I suppose that's what draws the line between males and females.

Troy was 19 when he wrote this story. He attended SUNY-Purchase and graduate school at Touro College, and became a high school principal in New York City.

Freddy Bruce

Wearing My True Colors

By Divine Strickland

When I was young, I preferred my sister's Barbie dolls to my Hot Wheels cars. "Your older brother never played with Barbies," my father said to me. But I didn't care; I was having fun. I never understood why other people had a problem with it.

As I got older, more people started to raise their eyebrows at my idea of fun. When I played double dutch with the girls instead of basketball with the boys, some of the boys would look at me like I was doing something wrong. But I never paid them any mind. That is, until around the age of 13, when things suddenly got worse.

When I was in 6th grade, I realized that I was attracted to a few boys at school. I knew then that I was gay, and I also knew I had to hide it. I didn't want to get myself into any drama. But even though I didn't tell anyone about my sexual orientation, it started to show.

I wore tight-fitting jeans and hung out with a group of girls. The way they carried themselves began to rub off on me. I had a switch in my walk and not much bass in my voice.

That's when the name-calling began. I got called every name in the book, like "homo" and "faggot." Even my family would make jokes about my feminine ways. They never intended to hurt me, but they did. I was depressed and confused about how people were treating me. It made me think that being gay was never accepted.

When I was about 14, my family started asking, "Are you gay?" I thought to myself, "Are they going to treat me differently if I tell them?" So I answered the one question everyone was asking with a lie. I said no.

But people still teased me because of how I dressed and behaved. Sometimes I would have to make my way around a group of guys to prevent them from saying something or even harming me. Other times, I defended myself and fought. By the time I got to high school, I was tired of avoiding people and fighting them. Something had to change.

I knew then that I was gay, and I also knew I had to hide it.

In freshman year of high school, I had a few gay friends who were seniors and I confided in them about my sexual orientation. One of them told me, "Trust me, once you come out of the closet, you're going to feel so much better about yourself." I decided I was ready to tell the people closest to me, even though I was scared about how they might react.

When I came out to my family and friends, I was shocked at their responses. "I been knew," is what they all said. Later they explained that it showed in the way I acted. I was glad that my family accepted my sexuality and still loved me no matter what.

But not everyone accepted me. Even though I felt happier and more confident now that I was out of the closet, it still upset me whenever I got harassed for how I looked and dressed.

One day, I was sitting on the subway with my friend Vera when suddenly, a woman started yelling about how none of the men on the train were giving up their seats for another lady who was standing with a child. Any other time I would have given up my seat for the child, but on this particular day my feet were killing me.

I looked at Vera and we both laughed at the crazy woman screaming on the train. It wasn't until she stood directly in front of me and yelled, "What kind of man are you?" that I realized she was talking to me, despite the fact that none of the other men on the train had given up their seats, either.

"Excuse me, who are you talking to?" I said.

"Men don't wear tight jeans and argue with women, so it's obvious that you are not a man," she said.

I stood up to get in her face and she took her hand and pushed me in my face. Before I could do anything else, a man on the train grabbed me and said, "Chill, she still a female yo."

I yelled at the lady, "I swear if I was wearing a du-rag and had my pants hanging off my butt, you never would've said anything to me, let alone put your hands on me."

I was embarrassed and angry. I felt like she took advantage of me because she had an idea that I was gay and thought I wouldn't fight back. I was tired of getting bad vibes from people just because of how I looked. Eventually, I even started getting criticized by someone I never thought would judge me: my own boyfriend.

I met Eric (not his real name) when I was 15 and he was 18. He didn't look like the type of guy who would go out with boys. We met in McDonald's, where he approached me in a strange way. He made it seem like he knew me already and wanted to get with one of my female friends. Later I realized he did this because he didn't want anyone to know he was gay, or, as he said, bisexual.

Eric became my first boyfriend and my first love. I never imagined that someone in the world would love me other than my family. I loved him, too. Even my family loved him. The only problem was that he wasn't out about his sexuality to anyone besides my family and me. It made me feel like our relationship was a secret.

Then one day, out of nowhere, he told me I was too feminine. He thought my tight, bright clothes were too much. Because I loved him so much, I was willing to change for him. I was getting tired of the comments from strangers anyway, and I figured maybe it was time to tone down my look. I stopped getting my eyebrows done and began to wear darker-colored clothes and looser jeans.

"Men don't wear tight jeans and argue with women, so it's obvious that you are not a man," she said

But I felt weird about changing who I was just to satisfy others. I didn't feel like myself when I wore baggy jeans. And I soon found out that changing my clothes wouldn't change how people saw me or treated me anyway.

One night Eric and I went to a community center party in our neighborhood. When the community center staff turned away some disrespectful guys at the door, the guys made a threat. "Any faggot that comes out is getting beat the hell out of," one of them said.

When the party was over, the only people left were all the gay guys and the staff. "It's time for you all to leave. We have to close the center," one of the staff members said. I could see the large group of boys waiting outside. I was nervous, but all that was left to do was leave. I walked outside with Eric right behind me.

"Hit them faggots!" the guys began to yell. Three shadows ran up behind me and when I turned around, one of the boys tried to punch me in the face. I jumped back and began fighting. I was nervous because one of my biggest fears was to get jumped by a group of boys. But I fought so hard that I barely got hit by any of them.

I looked around for Eric and I saw him fighting in the middle of the street. He was fighting five or six boys and none of them could even reach his face to hit him because Eric is 6'2" and they all were too short.

"Y'all getting killed by two faggots," people shouted as they watched the fight. I guess the boys' pride was beginning to hurt because in a quick second, they pulled out two guns and pointed them at Eric and me. I was so scared, I couldn't move.

"Divine, run!" Eric shouted. We ran. They chased us briefly but quickly gave up. I was in total shock that my life was almost over so fast just because someone was homophobic. That's when I realized that it didn't matter if I changed how I dressed or acted. I was wearing a pair of baggy True Religion jeans and an eight-ball leather jacket, and they still knew. People were still going to treat me the same way because I could never completely hide who I was. And I didn't want to.

I decided that instead of changing my appearance to make my boyfriend and a bunch of strangers happy, I needed to do what was going to make me happy. I went back to being myself, with my bright clothes and a switch in my walk. (Eric and I eventually went our separate ways, but remained friends.)

To this day, people continue to make rude comments toward me, and I know I'll keep encountering that. But there's something new about me now: I don't care.

About a year ago, a man shouted at me, "God did not make Adam and Steve, he made Adam and Eve" as I was walking to work one afternoon. People on the street looked at me, fearful about how I was going to react. Although I was embarrassed at first, I just giggled and proceeded on my way. I choose not to answer people like this back because I figure a person can't have a fight with himself.

When people say negative things to me, chances are I've already heard it, so I just laugh it off. In my head I think they have no type of style. Besides, my clothes get me a lot of compliments, too. Now I love when people stare at me because of what I have on. I even made up my very own saying, based on people staring at me: "Don't laugh at me because I'm different; laugh because you're the same."

I know that some people who want me to change my look are doing it out of love. My mother worries that many people will want to harm me for being gay. She says that me wearing tight, bright clothes is like wearing a sign that says, "I'm gay!"

I 100% understand and respect how she feels. She is a parent and parents are going to be concerned about their children's safety. But it has taken me too long to get where I am now to move back 10 spaces like I am playing Monopoly. I can't go through my whole life trying to make others happy.

Ever since I began doing things the way I wanted to, my self-esteem has risen. I'm happy with the way I dress and who I am. I refuse to change for someone else, whether it's a boyfriend or a stranger. As far as I'm concerned, you either love me or leave me alone.

Divine was 19 when he wrote this story.

Edward Cortez

From Shy Guy
to Smooth Talker

By Juelz Long

One summer when I was 13, I was in Maryland visiting my uncle Frank. We were in the car when we saw two cute girls standing at a hot dog stand. My uncle said, "You should get out and go talk to them." I'd been bragging all summer about how good I was with the ladies.

"I don't even know them," I said.

"That's the whole point," he laughed. "You should get to know them."

The girls were getting ready to pay for their hot dogs and leave. I was nervous and afraid of getting rejected.

"Come on," he continued. "You're always bragging about how you have all these phone numbers in your phone book. Let me see what you got."

"They're not my type, I can tell," I said. "And they probably have boyfriends already."

"Yo, you're scared," he said. "Let me find out my little nephew is scared of girls. Aww, dude, you can't be rolling with me with that kind of attitude, for real!"

I was hurt. It was embarrassing to have my uncle, an adult I trusted and respected, think of me that way. I knew if he would say something like that to me, my friends would do the same. I decided I had to change my ways. I had to become the person I'd bragged about being all summer.

I was a shy, clumsy, embarrassed boy without a clue. A lot of my classmates were already taking girls out on dates, walking them home and telling them they loved them. I'd never done any of that. There were times I didn't even walk in the direction of females because I knew I'd start tripping over my feet.

Meanwhile, my older brother and his friends were always talking about girls and how many numbers they'd gotten. Girls would shout to them, "Call me, sexy," and I'd wonder how it would feel if the girls were talking to me.

I wondered if I could learn how to be like my brother and his friends. I began to pay closer attention when I was with them. Instead of running my mouth like I'd done with my uncle, I did less talking and more listening.

One day my older brother Shawn and I were walking to the mall. "Umm, you see that?" he said. I looked around and saw a gorgeous young lady walking on our side of the street.

"Yeah boy, I see that," I said. "That's a dime right there." She had long hair, caramel skin, and hazel eyes. She was the type I imagined would be escorted by Puff Daddy or Jay-Z, not walking on an ordinary block in the Bronx looking beautiful. How in the hell would I approach a girl like that?

Then out of nowhere my brother said, "You're looking very beautiful today, sweetheart. Bless you much." My heart skipped a beat. What was he thinking? He didn't even know this girl.

But to my surprise, the girl stopped and turned around with a huge smile. "Thank you, boo," she replied. "You're not looking too bad yourself."

"No need to thank me, sweetheart, just giving credit where it's due," he said with such smoothness and confidence. "By the way, my name is Shawn."

"I'm Cookie," she said. She was still smiling, letting the sunlight beam into her pretty white teeth. "And what's your name, cutie?" she asked me.

I told her my name so quietly I had to repeat myself. Then I said, "I'll be back, I'm going to

> **I told myself that next time I would be the man and face the woman.**

the store." I went into a store to glue my face back together. As I walked away I thought, "What the hell is wrong with you? What was with all the low talking and stuttering?"

After that, I began asking all my older guy friends what to do in different situations, like when a girl flirted with me, or when I was interested in a girl but didn't have the courage to approach her.

One guy would say, "Don't think about what you're going to say to her, because you'll get discouraged and back down." Another guy would say, "Try to get some eye contact and let the body language talk." My favorite suggestion was to make her laugh and let her talk. I liked that because I love to make people laugh. It seemed like something I could do.

I realized I was getting different advice because each guy had his own style. I needed to find my own style, too. I didn't want to say I had a lot of money when I didn't, or that I drove a nice car when I didn't have a license. I wanted to be myself.

The next summer, I was sitting on a bench in an amusement park when I saw a girl with a bunch of her friends standing next to the ice cream stand. I stared at her and she kept looking back to make sure I was still looking. Then she whispered something to her friend and her friend came over to me.

"Hi," the girl said in a sweet, soft voice. She sounded like she was about 10 years old. "My aunt wanted to know how old you are," she said.

"Who's your aunt?" I replied.

"The girl with the red and blue shirt standing next to the balloons," she answered.

That was the girl I had my eye on. "Oh wow, she's your aunt? Tell her I said to holla at me."

But I was too shy to go over to the girl because she was with so many friends. I felt like I'd failed the test I'd studied so hard for. Shyness had always been my biggest obstacle. I told myself that next time I would be the man and face the woman.

I finally got a chance to put what I'd learned into action last summer, when I went on a cruise with my family for a week. I was leaving the game room on the ship one day when a girl was coming in. She was staring me directly in my face. I went past her and looked back and she was still looking at me and smiling. I stopped and said to myself, "This is my chance. Now or never."

I went back inside and sat down but she didn't see me. I remembered how my older brother used to hiss at a girl to get her attention. I always thought that was disrespectful, but I didn't want to think about right and wrong now.

"Psss," I hissed at her, my heart making the hardest pound I'd ever felt against my chest. I was really nervous because I doubted that I was doing the right thing and I didn't want to get played. "Psss," I hissed again, even louder. She looked around with a great expression of curiosity on her face.

"Stop acting like you don't see me," I said, smiling with sudden confidence.

"Oh wow," she said, bursting out in laughter. "I'm so sorry. I didn't see you sitting there. I'm so embarrassed," she said as she started heading toward me.

"No need to feel embarrassed." I said. "Well, maybe just a

little bit."

She started laughing hysterically. "Oh, I see you got jokes, huh. What's your name, Mr. Jokester?" she said.

"Juelz, and yours?" I asked.

"Christine," she replied. When she sat down next to me, I felt my heart going back to its normal speed.

In the end, I didn't hit it off with Christine, but we became good friends throughout the week. For the first time I felt confidence in myself, knowing I was doing things my own way.

I learned that my style was easy-going and laid back. I remembered how my older

I was really nervous because I didn't want to get played.

brother gave Cookie a compliment—that was his approach. Mine was making Christine laugh.

Now I'm 18 and still learning, but I find that I'm a role model for my younger cousins and friends. When they ask me the same questions I asked when I was their age, I tell them it's OK to be shy and that they should just be themselves. That's when I realize how far I've come and how much I've learned about the ladies.

Juelz was 18 when he wrote this story.

Emilia Martinez

Man With a Plan

By Michael Orr

I'd been living at my residential treatment center (RTC) about a month, having fun and not worrying about anything, when I met Earl. He was one of the resident troublemakers, in and out of jail all the time.

When the staff workers introduced him to me, he stuck his hand out to give me a pound and said, "What's good?" I gave him a pound and told him I was chilling out and relaxing. Then as I went walking toward the living room, he turned me around and sucker punched me out of nowhere. We were fighting for at least 10 minutes before staff broke us up. I had a busted upper lip from this dude and I didn't even know why he wanted to fight.

Earl was a Crip, the only one on campus. He was outnumbered one to two or three dozen, but that didn't stop him from representing his colors. Earl kept on causing trouble with everybody until he turned 21. In New York, that's when you "age out" and have to leave foster care and live on your own. Earl had no family, no friends and no place to go or live. We all witnessed that day when staff handed him some plastic bags and subway fare, wished him a happy birthday (talk about adding insult to injury) and sent him with his belongings to a shelter.

I didn't feel bad for him at all because he brought it on himself. The thing that got me was how they sent him on his way. I was really upset about their actions

Seeing what happened to Earl made me determined not to become another trapped statistic of the system.

because I pictured myself in Earl's shoes for that moment. I knew the administration workers were grimy, but what they did to that fool was messed up.

Maybe they had this planned just for him. Or maybe it applied to anyone who had no place to go. All I knew was I wasn't going to let it happen to me.

When I first got put in foster care at 13, I thought I wasn't going to be there long and I wanted to go back with my family. Then I started noticing kids getting discharged to their families and ending up back in foster care a month or two later. I decided then to make the best of foster care. Years later, seeing what happened to Earl made me determined not to become another trapped statistic of the system.

I had a job on campus in the cafeteria. It only paid $25 a week, but I began to put every cent I earned away and started thinking about living on my own. I knew the sooner I started, the better it would be for me.

I was 17 years old when they kicked Earl out. I was going to be 18 in three months so I felt I would be their next target. I had to get on my grind ASAP.

My social worker tried to convince me to go to a group home every time he had a chance, but I refused. I wanted to go straight to an Independent Living (IL) house, not a group home. (IL is a program that teaches teens who are aging out of foster care how to live on their own.)

At the RTC, there were people smoking, drinking, male staff having sex with female residents, people stealing from each other and lots of fights. I had no privacy. In IL I would be one step closer to being on my own. To qualify, I'd have to have a job or be going to college or vocational school.

One of my school advisers introduced me to a program called Vesid, which helps teens and adults find work or pays for them to go to school. I didn't know what field I'd be interested in, but since I had worked in the cafeteria my school advisor suggested I study culinary arts. I decided to give it a shot.

I had to complete the course in three months to get my certificate. But after two and a half months I quit to play my final year on the varsity basketball team. Basketball was one of the few things that kept me motivated and I loved playing.

When we discussed my future, I put on my serious face and told them my plan.

Then, during the course of my basketball season, my social worker assigned me to go to a group home, without telling me. That was a messed up surprise for me. I knew I needed to leave the RTC. I was getting older and it seemed like everyone else was getting younger. But I wanted to leave the way I planned with my workers from my agency. I'd lived at the RTC for almost five years, and it was a shock to have to leave everything all at once.

I was angry they had made a decision behind my back. I started thinking, "What was the point of having all those meetings if what I said was not going to make a difference?"

A few days after I moved, I had another meeting with staff. When we discussed my future, I put on my serious face and told them my plan to go to independent living and how good I had done on the campus. I even told them about what my social worker did and demanded they not pull that same stunt on me. They said I would be informed about any news that comes up about my future.

O n my 19th birthday I played my final game on the varsity team. Now I was ready to focus on getting a job and getting out of the group home. I prepared to find work at any place that was hiring.

I filled out applications at some stores but had no luck. My friend Jayvonne told me K-Mart was hiring, so I filled out an application. One week later, I went to an orientation and was handed a folder with my schedule inside. I walked back to the group home feeling surprised and proud of myself for getting a job.

About three months later, after my next meeting, I signed up for Section 8 (a program that gives you vouchers to help pay your rent) and a savings account. I had a job and stayed out of trouble. I completed all of the tasks they asked me to do with no problem, so there was no way they could deny me a spot on the IL list.

After six months, I was finally able to move to IL housing. When I received the news, I went nuts. I felt so great about it I started packing up my things immediately. The next day a van came to take me and my stuff to my new placement.

The only problem was that the new placement was right by campus, and I was afraid I'd be around the same people all the time. Sure enough, I arrived at the house to find lots of people from the campus hanging out. My new roommate had invited them to chill there and do whatever they wanted. They were drinking, smoking, and sleeping on blankets like it was a shelter.

There was never any privacy and it was always noisy at the house, so I dealt with it by spending most of my time at the b-ball court. A month or so later, I was moved to another IL house. I got my Section 8 vouchers and started searching for an apartment. I went to a real estate broker to help me find a place to live quickly before I left care.

He found a place that he wanted me to see, but when I got there the super had the wrong set of keys. I was tired and frustrated so I decided to stick with the place without seeing it. I signed a two-year lease, put down the first month's rent and security deposit and got the keys. When I went back to the apartment I was surprised to see how good it looked. I couldn't wait to move in.

My 21st birthday finally arrived and it was a breath of fresh air for me. I went to the IL office to get my grant money and the last of the money I was getting from the IL program. Then I celebrated my birthday and my accomplishment with my girlfriend Erica.

Now I've been living at my apartment for almost a year with Erica and things are going fine. I do some part-time work and I get to see my family more. I feel a lot better about myself, and I feel that Erica and I are changing for the better. I have grown into a mature young adult and I try to show my younger peers what they need to do after they get out of foster care.

At times I catch myself thinking about the decisions I made to get me to this point. If I had an opportunity to do it differently, I wouldn't change anything. To me the greatest thing about going from foster care to having my own place was the journey itself.

Michael was 21 when he wrote this story. He later married, had two children, and worked as a security guard.

Duran Rivera

My Secret Life
As an Opera Singer

By Jonathan Maseng

I'm a former opera singer, and proud of it. Opera charged my life and the way I look at the world, but at one point it wasn't something I was willing to share with people because I was too embarrassed. I was a secret opera man, hiding my pre-teen passion from my friends.

My career started in 4th grade when I joined my school chorus in Monticello, a town in upstate New York. One day my chorus master approached me about an opportunity. She said a friend of hers was the chorus master for the New York City and Metropolitan Opera's children's choruses. She asked if I'd be interested in trying out.

I was stunned. Opera? I'd never thought about that before. I thought opera was only about fat women in Viking costumes singing high notes in front of fake-looking sets.

But I told her that I was interested because, even though I had my doubts, I was secretly intrigued. I wanted to know what it'd be like to be onstage in front of so many people and sing. I wanted to see how a professional theater worked.

My dad brought me to the New York City Opera at Lincoln Center. I met several members of the children's chorus and sat in on rehearsal with them.

Then Ms. Horner, the chorus director, had me and another kid who was auditioning sing "America the Beautiful" and "Happy Birthday." When we were through, she told us to wait outside while she decided if we were in.

The minute I spent waiting was one of the longest minutes in my life. Opera didn't excite me yet, but I didn't want to fail a tryout and let down my chorus master. I sat in silence with the other kid until Ms. Horner came out.

"You're both in," she said. I breathed a sigh of relief. I didn't want to be a failure. I couldn't wait to tell my parents or my... friends?!?

I t hit me: I was an opera singer. What would I tell my friends? No kid I knew considered opera cool. I might as well say I'd become a yodeler. Chorus was one thing, but opera?

I thought my friends would think I was a sissy since many kids don't consider opera to be a "manly" occupation. And if they ever saw me on stage, I was sure I'd die.

I was a high alto, a girl's voice, and that made me self-conscious. I could just imagine my friends sitting in the audience and laughing when I'd sing, calling out, "Jon's a girl." I convinced myself that telling them meant certain ridicule.

When I got home, I told my mom I'd gotten in. She was happy and told me how proud she was. I felt a bit better about being in the opera.

My mom recognizing my talent made me happy, since, at the time, I waited for someone else's compliments to feel good about myself. That's why I was so worried about being rejected by my friends.

I was also insecure about school since I was the new kid there. I'd moved only a year before from Brooklyn, and I didn't have the kind of trust with my new friends as I had with people I'd known my whole life. I felt like an outsider and I figured that exposing my secret would make me feel even more alienated.

I told only my best friend that I'd joined the opera. He thought it was cool and wanted to tell other people, but I made him promise he wouldn't and he respected my wishes.

I was a secret opera man, hiding my pre-teen passion from my friends.

So every Tuesday in 5th grade, I'd leave school early and my dad would drive me two hours into the city for rehearsal. I told people I had business to attend to, but I didn't go into specifics.

Despite my shame in school, I had fun at rehearsals. I enjoyed going to the city and getting away from country life. I also made friends at the opera, becoming especially close with Nigel and Ray, two other members of the children's chorus.

When I would walk up to the security desk at the entrance and sign my name in the log book, I felt powerful, important. It was like I was part of the "in" crowd, which was unlike my experience at school.

But I felt torn between my life in the opera and my life outside it. When I was inside the opera house I felt strong, but away from it I felt like a loser for being an opera singer. I was living in two very different worlds, straddling their borders, and I didn't want to pull my foot out of either one. I didn't realize that it might be possible for those worlds to mix.

At the end of 5th grade, I moved back to the city and started going to a new elementary school. My old friends never found out about the opera. Even though I was glad my secret was safe, I wished I had felt comfortable enough with them to share my Lincoln Center experiences.

That year, I got my first parts in two shows: *Carmen* and *Tosca*. *Carmen* became my favorite opera to be in because the music was upbeat and there were plenty of fun props, like dulled-down knives.

I did the show several times over the years. The children's chorus was in the first and fourth acts. Between appearances, the other kids and I played games downstairs and ran around the maze-like hallways.

After the season ended that year (fall and spring seasons run about two to three months each), I kept in touch with Ray and Nigel by talking to them on the phone. I even went out to visit Nigel on Long Island a couple of times.

I also started to attend yet another new school after the break, the LAB school in Manhattan. I was still worried about how people would respond to my opera singing, so I kept it a secret.

When the new season began, I was cast in two new operas, *Carmina Burana* and *Attila*. I was happy that I'd be doing more performances, and I felt appreciated.

Inside the opera house I felt strong, but away from it I felt like a loser

Getting positive feedback on my work made me feel secure. I started to get less strict about my secret and I told close friends. Then, something happened that revealed my secret to everyone.

One day, I accidentally said something about "my friend from the opera" when I was talking to some students in the LAB lunchroom. They were shocked.

"Opera?" they said with wide eyes and stunned faces. My secret was out! I felt like I was going to hyperventilate. I tried to think of ways to slip out of it, but nothing came to mind. So I just gave in and told them the whole story. Surprisingly, they asked me questions about what it was like and the guys wanted to know how many "hot" girls there were.

Of course, after word got out, there were people who said

stuff like "You castrated?" but for the most part, my friends encouraged my singing. And so did strangers. People I didn't know were coming up to me in the halls and asking me to sing. It was a bit embarrassing since I didn't want so much attention, but it was better than being ridiculed. I would usually just go, "Ah, I don't want to," and they would let it be.

One time, though, my friends wouldn't leave me alone, so I broke down and sang something from *Carmen*. I hated it because I only liked to sing during performances or when it moved me, not at random. Still, after singing, they were like, "Oh, that's so cool!"

After all the years of keeping life at the opera secret, I felt like a big weight had been lifted from my shoulders. I didn't feel like I was lying to people about who I was anymore. I became more open and friendly, because I was less afraid of being teased.

I'd psyched myself out. I was so worried about what other people would think of me that I neglected to realize maybe they wouldn't say anything at all. Finding out that being in the opera wasn't such a big deal to other people made me feel stupid for feeling I needed to hide who I was.

Eventually, when my voice changed, I left the opera. And years later, I no longer feel the need to keep my old career secret. After dodging the truth, I learned that sometimes people build things up in their heads and make them bigger deals than they really are.

Jonathan was 16 when he wrote this story.
He majored in English at City College of New York.

Shaun Shishido

Why Be a Thug?

By Tyrone Vaden

Last week I was in a Chinese restaurant when an older guy came in. He was around 50 years old, and he looked like he could've been suffering from an illness because he was very thin and frail.

He was about to make his order when a guy who was around 28, 6' 2", and as big as refrigerator strutted in, pushed the older man out of the way, and yelled out his order. The older man turned to him and calmly said, "You could have waited your turn instead of rudely interrupting me."

The young guy gave him a cold stare and stormed out of the store. Later he came back in and started yelling at the cashier and cursing out the older man.

After the young man left again, the older man started talking to me because he knew that I had seen the whole thing. "Ignorance," he said "will get you nowhere. That guy thinks because he's younger than me that he can beat me. Tell me," he continued, "how are you just going to walk up to a man twice your age and disrespect him?"

"He's just ignorant," I told him, but I felt what the young guy was trying to do. He was trying to earn respect from the old man, but he was going about it the wrong way. The young guy was probably from the hood, and intimidation is a must in tha hood (or should I say on tha ave).

In the law of the streets, respect comes from putting fear in a man's heart so he won't challenge you. If a man can't intimidate others, the chances of him getting respect is 0-1.

It took me a long time to realize that violence isn't the key.

I used to be like that. I used to think that I could beat everyone and their mama. I wasn't like that because I wanted to fight, but because that was the only way I knew to get respect. It took me a long time to realize that violence isn't the key, but using your brain is. I'm calmer now.

Two years ago, when I'd just moved back to New York from Baltimore, I noticed thuggish behavior everywhere. In New York, people who have beef with each other argue for about a half an hour and then they fight, even if the problem could've been resolved by words. All that tells me is that they just want to fight.

At my first group home, we had a couple of guys who thought they were untouchable and that nothing would happen to them. You know how you have some guys who act the way they dress, like they wear baggy clothes and act loose. Well, they were as loose as they come. Yeah, they would dress jig, keep their money, and walk and talk like they were the hardest guys living.

They used to try to intimidate people by the way they talked, trying to be real thuggish. They used to pick on other guys in the group home who they knew would not defend themselves. They would shake these guys awake to make them go to the store at 2:00 in the morning, just to be mean.

They were so cruel that they would take advantage of people who were not on a violent tip, people who didn't know how to fight and didn't want to fight. I was disgusted at what they were doing.

After I was in New York for about seven months, I saw a kid in my old neighborhood walking to the store when two guys who were in the Latin Kings gang started picking on him.

"Yo, give me a dollar," they said.

The kid said, "I'm going to the store for my mother."

"So what," said the two Latin Kings, "give us all your money."

Now mind you, they were doing all of this in broad daylight in front of a lot of people. And when the kid wouldn't give the money to them, they jumped him and took his money. Damn!

A real man doesn't make a fool of himself by acting like a thug.

Maybe those guys want to be hard-core because they didn't have enough motherly affection when they were young. Maybe these guys are crying on the inside, wishing they had someone to love them. Or maybe they're just looking for attention and can't find positive attention, so they make themselves the center of everything by being "bad." If you ask me, they're not men. They're pitiful.

I overstand (not just understand) what a real man is. A real man isn't someone who plays hard and enjoys robbing, stealing, cheating, and fighting.

A real man doesn't pick on smaller kids for fun or resort to violence when a conflict could have been fixed through talking. Better yet, a real man doesn't make a fool of himself by acting like a thug.

The older guy from the Chinese store is a real man. He stood his ground, but had enough respect for himself not to waste much time or energy on the guy who was making a fool out of himself.

Like the older guy said: "Ignorance will get you nowhere." So will being a thug.

Tyrone was 18 when he wrote this story.

Frank Malkum

Skinniest Man in the Graveyard

By Anonymous

I never gave my weight a second thought until I was 9, when my parents sent me to a summer camp in upstate New York for one month. All summer I listened to the kids insult me about my weight.

"We can't let you on the bus. You won't fit and we'll crash on our way."

"If you swim, you'll eat all the fish and drink the whole ocean."

I felt like crap when they teased me, and usually I made a joke to take attention away from my weight. Or I'd make excuses, saying, "I'm not really fat. I'm just working out right now and need the extra weight to turn into muscle." When they didn't let up, I'd hit them with the hardest comeback I could, depending on what I knew about the kid who was teasing me, like: "Well, I'm not the one with no mom."

But sometimes I'd stay quiet, thinking, "He's right and I should be listening to him." I mean, I knew the kid was being mean, but I got the message loud and clear: being fat was unacceptable.

Today I know those kids who teased me were bullies, but back then I was so sad because I thought they were right. "How come I'm fat and can't do anything about it?" I thought. "I should be doing something."

After summer camp, I started 4th grade believing I was the fat kid because I had the big stomach and the boobies. I hated it because the other guys, the thin ones, were always jumping around and hanging out with the girls. I was always left out and I thought it was because of my weight.

Fortunately, I found some friends in that class who didn't judge kids who were different. They weren't fat, but they made me feel like my weight wasn't a problem.

But after school, I only thought about my weight. I weighed myself and looked at myself in the mirror three or four times a day. I used to walk on my toes around the house so I wouldn't hear how heavy I was when I walked. I'd lie down on my back and stretch really far, so it looked like I had no stomach at all.

I n Eastern Europe, where I was born, bigger was always better and food was the center of the family. So I ate a lot at home. And the food was hearty, tangy, and fulfilling. I especially loved my mom's special beef stroganoff recipe—strips of beef, beef stock, onions, mushrooms, and ketchup. Let me tell you, the entire dish was always gone within two hours, all because of me.

My grandmother always believed that I was too skinny for my age. At my grandmother's house, seconds and another helping for home were a must. The food was delicious and there was so much of it. I felt I was helping out by eating more so it didn't go to waste.

I don't want to put blame on everyone else, but the importance of food in my family overpowered me. And I've always liked more and more food, ever since I was a little kid. I felt that most people would put some food in their mouth and chew it over slowly, to get all the taste out of it. I shoveled—a little of this, a little of that, a little more. And when the plate was empty, I got more. I ate food like I breathed air.

When I was 13, I looked at my scale and it said 134 lbs. I was only about 5' tall and I couldn't believe how enormous I was. I wasn't just fat. I was huge. It was right there under my nose.

I didn't understand why I was fat. I thought, "I was always so nice to so many people—why would God let me become so huge?" Of course he didn't answer me and I wondered what was wrong with me. Because of my weight, I felt ugly and lonely.

I got the message loud and clear: being fat was unacceptable.

I didn't ask my parents for help with my weight, but I wish they had noticed and helped me do something about it. They could have helped me learn to stop when I was full so I wouldn't eat so much. If they'd only taken the food away from the table when we all had enough. But they didn't. When I was 14, my mom and dad just said, "Son, you've gained so much weight and you should lose it."

I eventually learned that there was a chart called the Body Mass Index (BMI), which showed you how much you should weigh depending on your height. I learned I was 50 pounds overweight for my height.

By the time I was 15, I decided it all had to go. I saw on TV that celebrities were losing weight by becoming bulimic or anorexic. I had no idea what that was, so I researched it online.

Then I starved myself as much as I possibly could. It's called anorexia and it was simple: you don't eat, so your body must eat itself (meaning its own fat, which I had plenty of).

I only did it for about three months, but oh man was I slimming down. I only ate bread and drank water every day, and I lost 40 pounds during that time. But my stomach felt as if a gremlin was inside and he was pushing and scratching at the walls to get out. Still, I loved the way I looked.

I also tried bulimia, which is essentially binge eating (overeating), followed by vomiting everything I'd just ingested. Once when I was 16, my grandma and I bought a huge amount of food at a Russian delicatessen. When it was all heated, I turned on the TV to *The Simpsons* and ate it all. Then I went into the bathroom, like I'd done so many times before, and blew it all out.

Throwing up was simple. Two fingers down the throat and out came all the crap that I regretted eating. But when I was done, it was disgusting. I smelled like throw up and my eyes were red from the pressure they'd just endured. I did it at least seven times a week.

Soon, I was throwing up almost all of my meals and I hated myself for it. I wanted to feel full and happy and eat things in moderate proportions. But I didn't think I had the strength to lose weight slowly by eating right and exercising a little every day. My feelings about the weight I was losing overwhelmed my feelings about how I was doing it.

Bulimia began to define me, and I did it until I was so skinny that I thought I was beautiful. I used to look at myself in the mirror. I had no boobs and almost no stomach and everything was tight.

My parents thought it was great, but they didn't know how I was losing the weight. I lied to them and said I was simply exercising more often. They never knew I was starving myself or throwing up my food.

But I knew I couldn't practice bulimia for my entire life. I knew it would have killed me eventually.

So once I was happy with my weight, in the summer of my 16th year, I decided to stop throwing up. It was much easier to eat and sit than to eat and throw up. Of course, without controlling what or how much I ate, I couldn't keep the weight down. By the time I was 17, I'd gained all of it back.

Now that I'm 18 years old and living on my own, I've decided it's time to take control of my body and my diet. I'm 6′ tall and I weigh 230 lbs. My ideal weight would be 175 (that's what I weighed when I was 16). That's 55 pounds to lose.

I know that to lose weight in a healthy way, I need to stay away from all the bad food out there. I could also eat slightly less when I do eat it. I could substitute tea and water for sugary drinks. And I've learned that things boiled or grilled are much healthier than frying. But I'm still not sure if I'm ready to change my eating and exercise habits to lose weight the right way.

Because of my weight, I felt ugly and lonely.

When I was offered the opportunity to interview Dr. Melissa Nishawala, an eating disorders specialist at the New York University Child Study Center, I happily accepted. I knew I wasn't going to venture out on my own and find out the facts about eating disorders. I decided to interview the psychiatrist mostly for my personal benefit.

She told me that anorexia can actually cause the brain to shrink. It also causes the body to shut down the production of white blood cells, which fight infections in the body. Bulimia can reduce the amount of potassium in your body, which can affect your heart rhythm and kill you. Throwing up also damages your stomach and esophagus and could cause them to rupture.

When I asked her if either disease could kill you, she said, "Both can be deadly, absolutely—10% of people die or maybe even more."

After talking to Dr. Nishawala, I decided that I'd never vomit or starve myself again. And I will warn people about the dangers of the disease. It's a self-inflicted disease and one of the dumbest things I ever did.

Dr. Nishawala convinced me that anorexia and bulimia would destroy me. And do I want that? No, I don't. I do not want to become the skinniest man in the graveyard.

The author was 19 when he wrote this story.

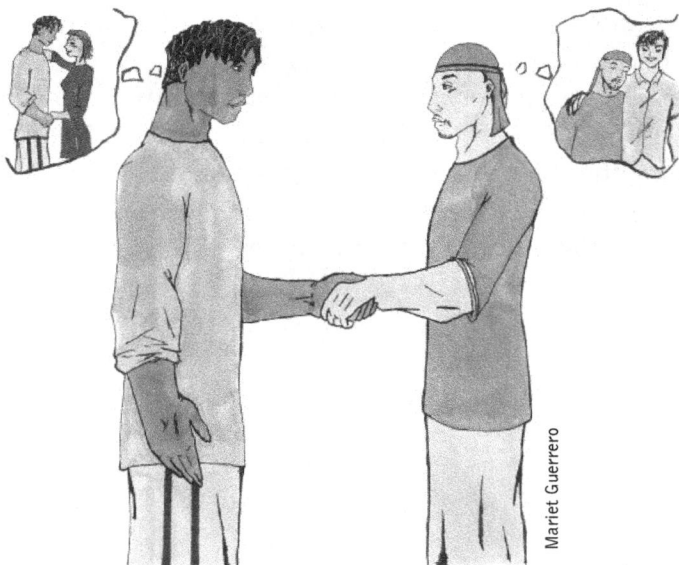

Mariet Guerrero

My Boy Wanted a Boyfriend

By Odé Manderson

One time I was within earshot of a conversation between two older guys and one of them had a friend who revealed he was gay. The dude responded by saying:

"I oughta kick your gay butt for telling me that. Get outta here."

Even though I'm straight, it makes my stomach turn to hear comments like that. Why would someone go out of their way to hate on people because of how they live their lives? I think it's an exercise in stupidity. But I don't feel comfortable going up to strangers and calling them out.

Still, I admit that I've used the word "fag" when I've wanted to insult someone's intelligence. No, I don't think gays are dumb, but it's a popular slang word. I know it's hypocritical and I'm trying to stop using the term, but old habits die hard.

And even though I don't consider myself to be homophobic, I used to think that gays act only one way because of how they're portrayed on TV and film. The actors who portray gays play it to the hilt with their bold sexual statements, style of dress, and comments about their gayness. Since I didn't usually run into anybody who acted in this way, I thought that gays would never cross my path. It was almost like they lived in a separate world.

I now realize I've probably been in contact with gays and didn't know it. In high school, my guidance counselor/college advisor mentioned in an off-hand manner during an assembly that he was gay. I didn't think too much about it, though. I still didn't think that I would ever meet someone like me, but gay.

Then, during my stint working in a summer jobs program two years ago, I met Thomas. On my first day of work he introduced himself to me and quickly became a good friend. He was different and cool. I learned a lot from him, like how to take action when times called for it and to speak my mind a lot more. He had a sense of humor, and he was straightforward about everything.

Evidently, he found me equally cool to be around. We started to hang out on the weekends. Sometimes we chilled at the mall. Other times we would hang out at a diner after picking up our paychecks. Or we would go to his cousin's crib, where we watched cable or listened to music.

When we were hanging out, I picked up on some signs that made me think Thomas might be gay, like the feminine quality of his voice and the way his hips swung back and forth when he walked. But I didn't want to jump to conclusions, so I never said anything about it. You can't tell someone's sexuality that easily. I couldn't assume Thomas was gay unless I heard it come straight from his mouth.

I didn't let it become a big issue with me. We were cool, so it didn't matter.

But toward the end of July, Thomas started to spend more

time alone. He went from being outspoken to quiet, and I started to wonder what was going on. I came home from work one day and the phone rang. It was him.

"What the hell is the matter with you?" I demanded. "Dyin' or something?"

He started to say something smart, but stopped. He sighed, then put down the receiver. A few seconds later someone picked it up.

"Hello?"

It was one of his cousins.

"Look," she started. "Thomas has something to say to you, but he's too shy to say it. Do you know what it is?"

I wasn't a total idiot. Or so I thought.

"Does it have anything to do with his sexual identity?" I asked calmly.

"Yes it does. That's not all, though. The reason why he had a hard time telling you was because he has a crush on you."

I tried to be very respectful of who Thomas was, even though I wasn't perfect at it.

I was shocked. Butterflies suddenly fluttered in my gut, then turned into wild hornets bursting through the wall of my stomach. I was silent for a moment before I decided to say something. I was prepared to hear him tell me he was gay, not that he had it for me.

His cousin said that he liked me because of my looks and personality. I blinked hard.

"Tell him he has nothing to be shy about," I replied, trying to compose myself. "Put him on the phone."

I heard a faint "here" as she passed the receiver to Thomas.

"Yeah."

"That's all you had to tell me? Look, you didn't have to tell me anything, so trusting me with that was strong of you. And this won't change our friendship, if that's what you're thinking. I'm cool."

Right after I hung up the phone with Thomas, I called my good friend Darnell because I needed some feedback and advice. The minute I explained what happened, he burst out laughing.

"Odé, that's the worst. He's in love with you, baaaaaa-beeeeeeeeee...." Then he added coldly: "I would've screamed on him."

"For what?" I said. "He knows where I stand, so it's not a problem. Plus, he's peoples."

"True, true," Darnell said. "I still would've screamed on him."

But I didn't want Thomas to feel bad that he'd told me. After hearing how kids our age treat gays—the threats, the jokes, and the violence—he was probably scared that I'd go and wild out.

After that, we still hung out as before, even though we didn't talk about his sexual identity or his crush on me again. I didn't want to bring anything up. I was thinking of how I would take it if I were gay and a straight friend started asking me about it. I thought that would make me feel uncomfortable. I didn't want to risk saying something stupid that would make Thomas feel uncomfortable.

I wanted to know if he was happy with himself, even though other people probably didn't accept him because he was gay. But I didn't ask. I didn't want to make him feel like he was on trial for being who he was. I also wondered if he still had a crush on me.

Knowing a guy had feelings for me was unsettling. When girls liked me, I felt a sense of satisfaction. But with Thomas, I felt bewildered. The idea of any guy liking me caught me off guard. This was a new experience and I felt uncomfortable. At the summer job where we worked, a lot of the employees caught on to Thomas' feminine mannerisms.

"Is he gay?" female counselors would ask me. Since I hung out with him, they turned to me for info.

"Yo, is that guy gay or somethin'?" the male counselors would ask. Then, answering themselves aloud, they'd add in disgust, "Yeah, he's gay." Most people only want to know if someone is gay so they can go in for the attack.

Because of attitudes like that, I think that gay teens are forced to live life differently than straight teens. They have to be careful about what they say and do in front of other people. So I tried to be very respectful of who Thomas was, even though I wasn't perfect at it. And Thomas would sometimes bring up stuff on his sexuality. Those talks let me know where he was coming from.

One time we started discussing relationships and we swapped stories. He said he had been involved in long-term relationships and his boyfriends were usually four to five years older than him. He talked about how guys treated him and how he felt about the person he was dating, but he didn't go into too much detail. I didn't ask for more information because I didn't want to overstep my boundaries as a friend, and I think he knew that.

For the rest of August, we hung out as much as we used to before Thomas came out. The only time I felt uncomfortable was when I let my tongue slip and used the word "fag" around him. I wanted to kick myself because I didn't know how Thomas took it. It didn't seem to bother him, and that really threw me off. It made me feel stupid, because I knew it was disrespectful. I think he understood that when I used the term it wasn't directed at him. Nevertheless, I didn't want to seem insensitive to him.

After a while I stopped wondering if he still had a crush on me. It didn't matter. Even if he still had feelings for me, it wasn't changing our friendship. But when the summer ended, we didn't keep in touch. A few weeks later, I began lifeguard training and went back to school and dated a few girls. He was trying to get a good job. We weren't able to chill as much because we had less time. After school started, he called twice to see how I was doing but he didn't ask to hang out. Neither did I. I figured he just didn't want to hang out anymore. I don't know why.

Even though we're not friends anymore, I'm glad that Thomas had the guts to come out. I'm impressed that he kept it real and revealed who he was. And our friendship showed me how my perceptions of gay people were pretty off. In reality, signs of gayness are nowhere near as cut and dried as they seem on TV because gay people don't all act the same.

Thomas made me realize that gay people aren't that different from straight people and can't be stereotyped. Thomas had some of the stereotypes

Knowing a guy had feelings for me was unsettling.

in the way he walked and talked, but he was also quiet and thoughtful. He wasn't loud at all. He couldn't even tell me about his sexuality himself.

I've realized I don't live in a separate world from gay people and I don't want to discriminate against them. Ten years from now a gay person could be my boss or my son's godfather. For all I know, my son could be gay. And I wouldn't love him any less.

Odé was 17 when he wrote this story.
He attended college and majored in writing.

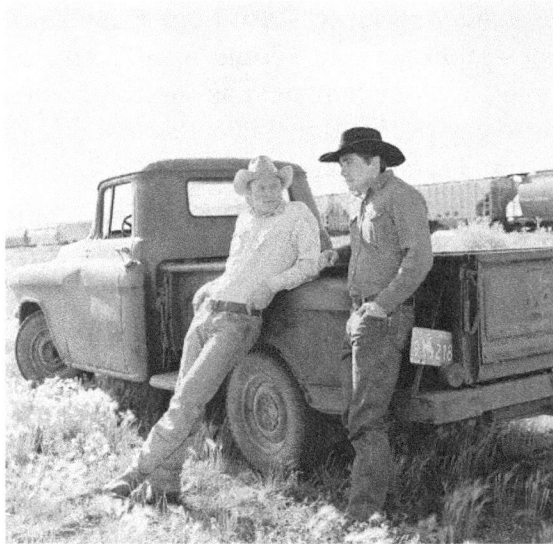

Focus Features

Brokeback Breaks Hearts —and Stereotypes

By David Schmutzer

When I first heard about "Brokeback Mountain" in my English class, my teacher wasn't referring to the movie. She was talking about the short story by Annie Proulx about two cowboys in love. The story inspired the movie. My teacher told us to read the story and highlight what parts we thought best captured the love between Jack and Ennis, the two main (male) characters. Some people chose lines the characters said, while others focused

---

Brokeback Mountain *is an Academy Award-winning film about the romantic and sexual relationship between two cowboys in the American West. It was nominated for eight Academy Awards and won three, along with many other film honors. In this article, David describes his reaction to the film.*

on explicit sexual descriptions.

When we discussed the relationship between the two men in class, a few kids giggled at the love scenes. One quote that sparked laughter was when Jack says to Ennis, "Why can't I quit you?" I wasn't surprised by their behavior. The students who laughed were still stuck in 4th grade, a time when many kids think being gay is funny and wrong.

> *The story breaks common stereotypes about gay men—the main characters are masculine cowboys*

I thought "Brokeback Mountain" was a powerful and provocative story. It breaks common stereotypes about gay men—the main characters are masculine cowboys—and it's moving. When the book was turned into a movie, there was a lot of controversy about showing a loving relationship between two men. I felt the movie was something I had to see so I could form my own opinions.

In the movie, like the book, Jack and Ennis meet one summer in the 1960s while herding sheep together on Brokeback Mountain and fall in love. At first they're hesitant and uneasy about expressing their feelings for each other, but slowly they allow their emotions to take over.

After the summer, Ennis (played by Heath Ledger) marries his fiancé, and Jack (played by Jake Gyllenhaal) eventually meets a woman whom he gets pregnant and marries. The men try to deny their emotions for each other for a while, but they can't stay apart.

For the next 20 years, the men continue to meet secretly every few months to quench their desire for one another. They leave their families periodically to continue their love, telling their wives they're going fishing together. Both still try to be husbands and fathers to their families because they want to be straight, but they suffer trying to accomplish that task. And they always return to Brokeback Mountain, the place where they first met.

One scene that vividly stuck out was at the end of their first summer together. It depicts their emotions bubbling up inside them—a mix of loving each other and hating the homosexuality that they've stumbled upon. To express this, they get in a fist-fight in order to be manly and not be gay. But their love for one another eventually emerges.

I already thought there was nothing wrong with being gay before I saw the movie. I believe that within 10 years, gay rights will have been recognized and people will realize how ignorant it was to discriminate based on sexual orientation, just like segregation is viewed now. (Of course, there will still be homophobes who linger on in future generations, just like there are still racists today.)

Still, I was unsure how far Ang Lee, the movie's director, would go to show the love between the two men. When I first saw where some scenes were headed, I felt a bit peculiar because gay sex is something that isn't often shown in books or movies.

But after I saw those scenes, I felt fine. I've always believed that love between two people of the same sex is entirely natural. I thought of the love scenes between Jack and Ennis the same way I think of love scenes between a man and a woman: just part of the movie.

I know many teens, including a couple of classmates at school, are apprehensive about reading a story or seeing a film like *Brokeback Mountain*. They think it's gross because ever since elementary school, the words "gay" and "faggot" have been thrown around as insults. They associate being gay with being lewd and immoral, even though it's as predetermined as being male or female.

I thought portraying gay people as cowboys was a great way to show there's no shame in homosexuality, since cowboys are considered the pinnacle of manliness. The movie will help people dismiss feminine stereotypes about gay men. Jack and Ennis drink and smoke like many straight men do.

Brokeback Mountain was great for many reasons, from the cinematography to the acting to the costume design. I recommend it to anyone, especially someone who's uncomfortable with homosexuality. Reading the short story or seeing the movie could make you think twice about your feelings. It's a love story. So what if it's between two men?

David was 16 when he wrote this story.
He later attended the University of Chicago.

Rosa Perin

Messing Around's
No Match for Love

By Christian Galindo

As a guy, I once thought that going out with a lot of girls was cool. I think I got that belief from my cousin Jimmy. He's five years older than me and I've always looked up to him, even though we've now lost contact.

My cousin was a "dog." He fooled around and slept with many girls, which made me think that's how guys naturally are. When I was 13, I distinctly remember him telling me, "Chris, you shouldn't fall in love with any girl just like that. Play around. Enjoy your life." He said that getting serious with a girl would cause me problems.

During that time, I'd already started dating girls here and there, but I was mostly dedicated to my schoolwork and didn't think about girls that much.

But as I got older, I became more interested in the opposite sex. After I turned 14, I got involved with Jane. We messed around for about a week.

Then in April, more than two months after I'd stopped seeing Jane, I met Kate. We hung out a lot and messed around, but to me it wasn't serious. I only told a few people in school that we were together because I still wanted to go out with other girls from school. Kate and I often argued about my refusal to commit to her. We stopped dating after a month and a half.

I was trying to follow Jimmy's advice, trying to have fun and not complicate my life. Besides, the girls I'd messed around with were conceited. I didn't want to get seriously involved with girls who had that type of personality.

Then I met Daisy at a party one summer. She was 18, visiting New York from another city. We fell for each other and ended up having sex three days after we met. She went back home soon afterward. I was infatuated with her because she was attractive and sweet. I felt more for her than any other girl I'd been with before.

But I didn't love her. The distance was too much. I eventually told her that we both needed to see people who lived in our cities. I felt bad

Looking at Paula, I felt hypnotized.

about ending our relationship because she sounded hurt when I broke it off. It seemed like Jimmy was right—relationships caused problems.

But, again, remembering his words, I figured that I'd feel better by seeing other girls. Sure enough, after two weeks, I met other girls who I had fun with.

Then, one day during the fall semester of 10th grade, I went up to my friend Angela in the hallway to say "hi." As she opened her locker, I noticed this girl next to her. She had the face of an angel.

"Christian, this is Paula," Angela said. "She's new in school."

Looking at Paula, I felt hypnotized. "Nice to meet you,

Christian," she said.

"Nice to meet you, too," I said. "I guess I'll be seeing you around." From then on, I stopped and talked to Paula whenever I saw her in the hallway. We soon became friends.

I felt very attracted to Paula. She has a heavenly face and shapely body, but most important, she's down to earth and natural. She rarely wears makeup, preferring Chapstick over lipstick. She's friendly and helps people out, unlike some of the girls I'd gone out with.

Those girls wouldn't even talk to some of their friends on days when they thought they looked too good for them. They often wore tight jeans to show their butts and get guys' attention.

Well, that's how they got mine, but I still preferred Paula's style. Even when she wore tight jeans, she didn't seem to be showing off. I'd never gotten to know a girl like Paula. I wanted to spend more time with her. I wanted to be her boyfriend. I felt like I had to disregard Jimmy's advice, because my heart told me I should be with her.

Being serious has helped me to discover what love's about.

I told Angela that I liked Paula a lot. Angela said that Paula cared more about a guy's personality than his looks. So I asked Paula to be my girlfriend three months after we met, hoping she liked my personality.

She said she had to think about it. A week later, Paula told me she didn't want to be my girlfriend because she didn't know me well enough. I felt bad, because I liked her so much. But I accepted her decision.

During the summer I still thought about Paula, but rarely saw her. But during the beginning of 11th grade, I started to talk with her during my free time after school. Over the weeks, she became my best friend. I still wanted Paula to be with me, but didn't want to mess up the beautiful friendship we'd established.

When our school's Halloween dance came up I invited Paula,

just as a friend. But something was different that night. We were dancing in the middle of our darkened cafeteria. Red, green, and blue lights shone across Paula's face from a disco ball. Suddenly, she hugged me. I was surprised. I hugged her back. Then we kissed.

It didn't feel real. I thought I was dreaming. But then I realized that this meant she'd be my girlfriend. After we kissed, I asked her again to be my girlfriend, and she said "yes." I was overjoyed.

Over the next few weeks, I discovered how good it felt to have Paula be such a huge part of my life. Everyone in school soon knew we were a couple. One of my counselors referred to her as my "wife" because he always saw her with me.

We started cooking and doing homework together. I also introduced Paula to my mother and grandmother, which I'd never done with any of my previous girls.

But I was scared. I realized I was starting to fall in love with Paula, and I felt like I was showing her more love than she was showing me. I soon told her I was starting to fall in love with her and that I wanted to know if she felt the same way too. I told her I feared that she'd hurt me because she wouldn't care for me as much as I cared for her.

She said that I had to trust her. "I'm also falling in love with you," she said. "Let's just let time do its work." Her words were a relief. I agreed to see what would happen.

I realized that being in a serious relationship is far more important to me than messing around. Being serious has helped me to discover what love's about.

Without knowing Paula on a deeper level, I wouldn't be able to experience what it's like to trust my girlfriend and feel supported unconditionally. I feel much happier being so close to someone than when I was just messing around.

But we've also had conflicts. Paula can be very stubborn and often wants to do things her own way. When we had disagreements, she argued her points even when she knew I was right.

I felt confused. I wanted to be with her, but felt like I'd resent her if I continued dealing with her attitude. So in March, I told her that if she kept being so stubborn, I'd prefer to break up. She immediately said she'd try to change.

And she has. She listens more to what I say and doesn't push her arguments as much as before.

We've also argued about the amount of time we spend together. I'm usually available on the weekends, which is when she has to do chores with her mother and complete her school-work. I get angry because I want to see her more, and my anger in turn makes her upset at me.

Even though I want to spend more time with her, I've realized she has other responsibilities in her life and she's doing all she can to see me. So I resolved not to get angry with her over that issue anymore, particularly since I'm only spoiling our quality time.

We communicate well with each other, which helps us get over our conflicts. So far, we've been together for six months.

I care a lot about Paula, as much as I care for myself, and sometimes even more than that. When she's sick, I wish I could be sick in her place. I never thought that I could love someone so much.

I know some guys will still say that being a player is the best way to be. But I know that, for me, messing around is no match for being in love.

Christian was 16 when he wrote this story.

Freddy Bruce

Barbershop Debates:
A Rite of Passage

By David Etienne

A few months ago, I went into the barbershop on my block for a haircut. My cousin and I were the only ones there under 20. Everyone else was talking about the two best NBA players right now: LeBron James and Kobe Bryant. One group said that Kobe was a better player than LeBron, and another group said LeBron was better.

Many people say that women gossip at beauty salons. I guess you can't call it gossiping, but men do talk a whole lot at the barbershop, mainly about sports and politics.

I sat there listening to them talk while the barber slowly cut my hair just like I had asked him to. I wanted to participate, but I felt like I was too young. It's rare to find a young kid in the barbershop speaking in the same conversation as the barbers and older customers.

In my head, I planned something to say about how LeBron James makes players around him play better and Kobe only cares about himself, not the team. But I said nothing because I was afraid no one would listen to me. When the barber was finished with my hair, I simply paid him and said thank you. I put on my jacket, and my cousin and I walked out.

A few weeks later, I went back to the barbershop for a shape-up. There weren't as many people there this time—only two barbers and three people waiting to get a haircut. And this time they weren't talking about sports, but about politics and the 2008 election.

They started by talking about a shooting that took place in the neighborhood, and the shooters were African-American. One of the barbers, a black man, said this kind of violence among black people was the reason a black man would never become president. That led to a discussion about Barack Obama and Hillary Clinton, and how history may be made in the United States this year.

Just like they had chosen sides between Kobe and LeBron, three of them chose Barack and the other two chose Hillary. Those who had chosen Hillary said that having her as president would be the same thing as having Bill Clinton as president.

"I am Trinidadian. I would love to see the first black president, but I really don't mind," one man said. "Matter fact, I don't even know if I'm voting yet."

My barber answered, "I'm sure that you're not going back to Trinidad any time soon, so the best thing to do is to vote for who will be controlling the place you live in for four years."

In a way I agreed with both men. As an immigrant, all my attention goes into trying to become somebody so I can go back to my country. And besides not being old enough to vote, I'm not yet a U.S. citizen. But as long as you're living here, it's best to have a say in who's representing you if you can.

One of the men said that if Obama was to become the president, his political enemies would do a lot of research on him, until they found some controversy big enough to get him thrown out of the White House.

I was thinking that any president who's hated by a group of people will be investigated this way no matter what. But I still didn't say anything.

I didn't want to share my point of view on the election as much as I had wanted to participate in the Kobe and LeBron conversation. Anytime there's a basketball game on you can expect me to be watching, but I don't really follow politics. Then, out of nowhere, my barber asked me who I think will make a better president, Barack or Hillary.

I thought for a moment. I was thinking that the unexpected is not the impossible, therefore anything can happen. So I answered,

I wanted to participate, but I felt like I was too young.

"Either one of them would make a good president. But don't be surprised if John McCain ends up winning the election." My barber agreed and began pointing out reasons why McCain is a strong candidate, like the fact that he's a former soldier.

After that, I didn't feel like the youngest person in the shop. I felt smart, because everybody agreed with me. I didn't say much else, but I walked out of the barbershop with a big smile in my heart and on my face. Next time I go in there, I won't be afraid to participate in any kind of conversation—it's more fun than just watching everyone else talk.

David was 17 when he wrote this story.

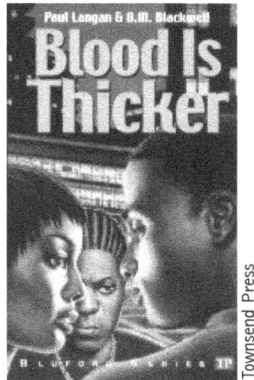

Blood is Thicker

"Goodbye, Darcy," Hakeem Randall said, gently letting go of Darcy Wills, his girlfriend for the past year. The tears in her eyes were like daggers slicing deep into his heart.

"Goodbye, Hakeem."

He watched her walk down the short driveway. If there was anything he could do to stop his family from moving away, he would have done it. But the decision was out of his hands.

Squinting under the Monday morning sun, Hakeem felt like someone had wrapped him in a heavy blanket of gloom. He wouldn't see Darcy again this summer. Maybe not ever. And in just a matter of hours, his old friends at Bluford High School and his home in southern California would be thousands of miles away.

"I'm gonna miss you, girl," he mumbled as Darcy turned the corner and disappeared. "You and everything else."

Here's the first chapter from *Blood Is Thicker*, by Paul Langan and D.M. Blackwell, a novel about teens facing difficult situations like the ones you read about in this book. *Blood Is Thicker* is one of many fiction books in the *Bluford Series*™ by Townsend Press.

Just weeks ago, his parents had informed him that they were moving the family to Detroit to live with Uncle James and Aunt Lorraine. The news struck Hakeem like a bomb blast, turning his world upside down overnight. Yet, as bad as it was, the announcement wasn't the worst thing he heard recently.

Five months ago, his father was diagnosed with kidney cancer. Surgery, chemotherapy, and the sickness it caused had reduced Dad's strength so much that he could no longer perform his job as a warehouse manager. For three months, Hakeem watched as his father's size diminished and his face aged. Though the treatment had stopped the disease, it left Dad a shadow of his former self, and it devastated the family's savings.

"We've spent everything we had on medical bills, baby," Mom said tearfully a few weeks ago. "I don't know what's gonna happen. But no matter what, I need you to be strong, Hakeem. I need you to be the man around here."

Hakeem nodded solemnly in response, expecting that the family would find a small apartment nearby. He was even ready to share a bedroom with his seven-year-old twin sisters so his parents could save money. But Hakeem never imagined that his Uncle James would invite the family to Detroit or that Dad would agree to go.

"I don't know what choice we have," Hakeem's father explained when he told the family the news. "Even though the cancer's stopped, the doctors say it could be months before I get my strength back. And without our savings, we can't afford to stay here any more," he said, massaging his forehead, his scratchy voice sounding much older than his forty years. "I wish I didn't have to do this to you. I'm sorry."

"Don't worry, Dad. It'll be all right," Hakeem had replied, half believing his words. Besides their money problems, Hakeem knew there was always a chance the cancer could return, a possibility which kept him up many nights, his heart racing with fear. In a few days, Dad would meet with doctors in Detroit to see if the cancer was still in remission.

Even though no one admitted it, Hakeem knew one reason Dad was moving them to Detroit was to keep his family together in case his health took a turn for the worse.

Watching the movers load his family's belongings into the storage truck, Hakeem felt as he had years earlier when someone robbed his church. The stolen money had been collected for a little girl who had leukemia, but that didn't stop the thieves from taking every cent. He had decided then that life was cruel. His father's cancer diagnosis, his horrific battle with the disease, and the sudden move were just the latest proof.

"You all right, Hakeem?" Dad asked, snapping Hakeem from his thoughts. "I know it isn't easy sayin' goodbye to your friends, especially Darcy."

"I'm fine, Dad. Darcy and I said what we had to say," Hakeem replied, trying to hide his sadness. *Be strong*, he reminded himself.

"That's it," his mother said as the movers closed the back of the truck. "Everything's packed, and the airport taxi is here. We gotta leave now. Come on, everyone."

Hakeem grabbed his suitcase, the notebook he used as a journal, and his old guitar, and took one last look at his house. Without furniture and pictures, it was a cold and empty shell, not the place where he grew up.

I can't believe I'm not coming back, he thought, glancing down the street toward his school, Bluford High, just a few blocks away.

I need you to be the man around here, his mother's words echoed in his mind. "Come on, son," his father urged. The family was waiting in the cab.

Hakeem took a deep breath, wiped his eyes, and said a silent goodbye to his world.

Good men beat down
Smiles turn to frowns
There is no logic

In a world so tragic

Hakeem read the words from his notebook. He had written them when his father first mentioned the move to Detroit. It seemed as if years had passed, not weeks. He flipped the page bitterly.

The dull hum of the plane's engines had lulled the rest of his family to sleep, but Hakeem could not relax. His mind swirled with thoughts of Darcy and his closest friends, Cooper and Tarah.

Maybe one day he'd write a song for them, he thought. Hakeem turned to a blank sheet of paper and stared at the tiny blue lines on the page. For years, he'd been singing and playing his guitar. He joined his church choir in second grade. Later, when he developed a stuttering problem in middle school, he discovered that it disappeared whenever he sang. Years ago, Mr. Smalley, the choir director, praised his voice.

"God gave you some talents, young man. Be sure you use them."

Hakeem hadn't sung for the church in years. But he did perform from time to time at Bluford. Even when he wasn't singing, he was always jotting lyrics in his notebook for songs he might sing one day. Music and writing were two things he relied on when the rest of the world was a mess. In his songs, he could control everything. There was no cancer. No goodbyes. Not unless he decided it.

Hakeem glanced at the notebook and tried to remember everything he knew about Detroit. He'd been there once before. It was ten years ago, when he was just six years old. Then, his father was to him the strongest person in the world. A person immune to disease, to cancer and chemotherapy. A superhero.

What Hakeem did most during the visit was eat huge dinners at his aunt and uncle's house and play video games with his cousin Savon. The two boys were nearly the same age, though Savon was much heavier.

"Savon's a husky boy," his mother used to say.

During the weeks he stayed in Detroit, Hakeem and Savon played for hours on end. Hakeem remembered once the two were playing catch in the street when some teens stole their ball.

"Thanks, Wimpy and Blimpy," the teens mocked as they strolled down the street, passing the ball around. The moment had stuck in Hakeem's mind. The teasing hurt, but it had also made him feel close to his cousin. They shared a special bond that moment. They were family.

But when Hakeem returned to California, he gradually lost touch with Savon. An awkward phone conversation three years ago at Christmas was the last time they talked. And now, after so many years, the dim memory of Detroit was bittersweet, a reminder of a past long gone.

Staring out of the small window next to his seat, Hakeem watched a veil of wispy clouds pass beneath him. His memories did little to erase the hole the move was carving into his life.

I miss home already, he thought, stretching back in his seat and closing his eyes.

I miss home.

"Are we there yet? Are we at Uncle James's house?" asked Charlene, one of Hakeem's younger twin sisters.

"Almost," Dad said wearily from the passenger seat of the rental car. Since Dad got sick, Mom drove the family everywhere.

"You've been asking that ever since we landed," snapped Charmaine, rolling her eyes at her sister. "Can't you just stop talking?"

Hakeem yawned and said nothing. The hour wait to get off the plane and pick up their bags was tiring. Now, the twenty-five minute drive through city traffic to Uncle James's house felt like slow torture. His sisters only made it worse.

"Is this it?" Charlene asked suddenly as the car stopped at a traffic light. "Is this where we're going to live at?"

"Shut up," Charmaine groaned.

"*Girls!*" Mom snapped. "If you don't stop whining, I'm gonna give you both somethin' to whine about."

"Make a right up there on Sawyer Street," Dad interrupted. His tired voice silenced everyone.

Outside, the houses were older and more densely packed than those back home. Made of red brick, many were row homes, though a few bigger houses did stand alone on some blocks. At the end of one street, Hakeem spotted a playground with a swing set and basketball court. A steel fence surrounded the park, making it look more like a prison yard than a playground.

Several teenage boys were shooting baskets as Hakeem and his family passed. One reminded Hakeem of his best friend, Cooper Hodden. Coop was one of the toughest people he knew, but he was also one of the nicest. When he found out that Hakeem was moving away, Coop had almost cried.

"Stay with *us*, Hak! My mom says we got room for you," he insisted. "Besides, she likes you more than she likes me."

For a second, Hakeem had considered Cooper's offer. He desperately wanted to stay, but he couldn't abandon his family. Not with everyone depending on him. Still, as he gazed out at the unfamiliar neighborhood, part of him wished he'd listened to Coop.

On a corner up ahead, Hakeem noticed two guys sitting on the steps of a house. One had a sharp angular face and wore a sideways baseball cap. The other was shaved bald and shirtless, his chest as wide as a barrel. Both glared at the car as the family approached.

Hakeem felt a nervous twinge in the pit of his stomach. Seeming to sense tension, Hakeem's mother pushed the accelerator, and the rented sedan lurched forward.

Welcome to the neighborhood, Hakeem thought bitterly to himself.

As they drove further up Sawyer Street, the homes gradually began to resemble what Hakeem remembered from his childhood. Some featured small porches with chairs and iron railings.

Others had driveways and tiny f ront yards lined with flowers. While an occasional house was boarded up and empty, most looked recently painted.

"One more block," Dad said, as the car passed two young boys racing each other along the sidewalk. Hakeem remembered how he and Savon had run up and down the streets years earlier. He wondered what his cousin would be like today.

Mom slowed the car to a stop in front of a green and white three-story house. "Here we are," she announced, her voice more relieved than excited.

"It's smaller than I remember it," Hakeem said.

"That's because you're bigger," Dad replied with a haggard smile. Though his face looked older, his intense black eyes were as clear as ever. "Looks like James had the house painted. The color's different," he added.

"How did you remember something like that?" Mom asked, unbuckling her seatbelt.

"My memory still works even if the rest of me ain't what it used to be. That house used to be bright yellow, kind of an eyesore. Good thing they repainted it." Dad chuckled then, a sound as scratchy and dry as sandpaper.

Hakeem cringed at Dad's raspy laughter, a scar of the illness that had threatened his father and driven them out of their home. Keeping his thoughts to himself, he stepped out onto the curb and scanned his new neighborhood.

At the end of the block, a fire hydrant gushed water into the street. In front of it, a crowd of children splashed loudly, their joyful screeches mocking Hakeem's mood. Somewhere far off, sirens screamed into the summer air, while overhead, a jet plane rumbled across the sky. Across the street, a mottled German shepherd growled menacingly from a nearby porch.

Hakeem shook his head at the strange chorus of sounds. He felt as if he'd just been dropped into the center of a strange and hostile world.

"They're here!" a husky voice called out from behind an open window. "It's about time."

Hakeem glanced up from the trunk and saw a muscular young man with tightly braided cornrows step out of the house and come toward his mother. He wore a white T-shirt and navy blue and white striped athletic pants. A thick silvery chain with a glimmering letter S hung from his neck. Hakeem didn't recognize him. "Savon? Is that you?" Hakeem's mother asked.

Savon? Hakeem's jaw dropped. It couldn't be. The person who stood before them looked nothing like the overweight kid from years earlier. Instead, he resembled a middleweight boxer.

"Who else would I be?" Savon asked, strutting down the short walkway with his thick arms swaying from side to side. "Wassup, Uncle Henry," Savon said, as he approached the car. "How you doin', Aunt Selma?"

Hakeem's mother threw her arms around Savon. "I can't believe my eyes, Savon. My Lord, I almost didn't even recognize you. You've grown into quite a young man."

"Well, that's what happens when you don't see somebody for ten years," Savon said proudly. "Last time you saw me I was just a chubby kid," he added.

"Ten years is too long for a family not to see each other," Hakeem's mother replied, shaking her head at her own comment. "Where does the time go? You kids grow up so fast."

"Aw, don't start gettin' sentimental on me, Auntie. Looks like we're gonna have lotsa time now," he added and then turned to Hakeem. "What up, cuz?" Savon asked, his eyes squinting slightly. "Now *you* don't look that different from back in the day. Maybe a little taller, that's all."

Hakeem could easily see over Savon's head. He had to be at least two inches taller than his cousin. But Savon was definitely more muscular—and probably stronger. Yet what struck Hakeem most about Savon was his eyes. They seemed almost angry. "Man, you always were skinny, cuz. But now you look like a toothpick,"

Savon added. Even his voice seemed to have a bitter edge.

Hakeem blinked for a second, unsure how to respond. Was his cousin kidding, or was he trying to start trouble?

"That's all right, Savon. I remember you being a little thick in the middle. Looks like some of that thickness left your stomach and went to your head," Hakeem replied playfully, trying to turn the moment into a joke. He then offered his hand to shake Savon's.

"I guess we can't all be as perfect as you, huh, cuz?" Savon said. There was an icy bite to his voice, and he ignored Hakeem's outstretched hand. "But it's all good 'cause while you spent years bein' everybody's favorite son, I spent some time hittin' the weights. And from what I see, weights would do your skinny butt some good," he snapped.

Hakeem swallowed hard. He was stunned, but no one seemed to hear the comment his cousin made. For an instant, he felt his old stutter beginning to seize him. Though the problem was nearly cured, it flared up when he was stressed or nervous. He shook his head and tried to think of a comeback.

Just then, his little sisters sprinted up to him, grabbing his arm.

"Mom said for you to unload the trunk," Charmaine said nervously.

Savon looked down at them then and laughed. "Oh no, you brought rugrats!" he exclaimed. "Two of them!"

"We ain't no rats," Charlene protested, "so don't be callin' us that."

"Don't get mad, I was just teasin' you," Savon said. "You better get used to that 'cause I do a lot of it."

Charlene frowned and moved closer to Hakeem, as if she was looking for protection. He put his hand on her shoulder. "It's okay, Charlene. He's just playin', that's all—"

"Oh, thank God you made it!" a woman's voice interrupted. "I been prayin' ever since you left California!"

Hakeem turned to see his Aunt Lorraine standing on the porch. She looked heavier than he remembered, but she still had a sweet, round face and a warm, inviting smile.

"And look at the toothpick they b rought with 'em," Savon laughed, pointing his finger at Hakeem. "Hakeem's as skinny as he was when we were kids," he added.

Hakeem seethed at the comment but smiled out of respect for his aunt.

"Oh, he's just fine," Aunt Lorraine said, waving Savon away with her hand. "And he's good-looking, too. I bet you had all the girls back home chasin' after you."

Hakeem blushed and shook his head as she came closer to him. "I do okay," he said, thinking of Darcy and their painful breakup.

Savon seemed to be annoyed at his mother's comment. He frowned and

stepped away while she approached. "I missed you, Aunt Lorraine," Hakeem said, giving her a hug.

"I missed you too, baby. It has been too long. Way too long. I keep telling myself that all this trouble is a blessing in disguise. It's a way for all of us to get to know each other again." Letting him go, she turned her attention to Hakeem's sisters. "And look at you two!" she cheered, wrapping them both in a massive embrace. "I am so happy to finally see you!"

Hakeem smiled, nearly forgetting the painful events that had forced them to Detroit.

"C'mon, Cali-boy." Savon's rough voice jarred him like an alarm clock. "We got work to do."

Blood is Thicker, *a Bluford Series™ novel, is reprinted with permission from Townsend Press. Copyright © 2002.*

Want to read more? This and other *Bluford Series*™ novels and paperbacks can be purchased for $1 each at www.townsendpress.com. Or tell an adult (like your teacher) that they can receive copies of *Blood is Thicker* for free if they order a class set of 15 or more copies of *Boys to Men*. To order, visit www.youthcomm.org or call 212-279-0708 x115.

Teens:
How to Get More Out of This Book

Self-help: The teens who wrote the stories in this book did so because they hope that telling their stories will help readers who are facing similar challenges. They want you to know that you are not alone, and that taking specific steps can help you manage or overcome very difficult situations. They've done their best to be clear about the actions that worked for them so you can see if they'll work for you.

Writing: You can also use the book to improve your writing skills. Each teen in this book wrote 5-10 drafts of his or her story before it was published. If you read the stories closely you'll see that the teens work to include a beginning, a middle, and an end, and good scenes, description, dialogue, and anecdotes (little stories). To improve your writing, take a look at how these writers construct their stories. Try some of their techniques in your own writing.

Reading: Finally, you'll notice that we include the first chapter from a Bluford Series novel in this book, alongside the true stories by teens. We hope you'll like it enough to continue reading. The more you read, the more you'll strengthen your reading skills. Teens at Youth Communication like the Bluford novels because they explore themes similar to those in their own stories. Your school may already have the Bluford books. If not, you can order them online for only $1.

Resources on the Web

We will occasionally post Think About It questions on our website, www.youthcomm.org, to accompany stories in this and other Youth Communication books. We try out the questions with teens and post the ones they like best. Many teens report that writing answers to those questions in a journal is very helpful.

How to Use This Book in Staff Training

Staff say that reading these stories gives them greater insight into what teens are thinking and feeling, and new strategies for working with them. You can help the staff you work with by using these stories as case studies.

Select one story to read in the group, and ask staff to identify and discuss the main issue facing the teen. There may be disagreement about this, based on the background and experience of staff. That is fine. One point of the exercise is that teens have complex lives and needs. Adults can probably be more effective if they don't focus too narrowly and can see several dimensions of their clients.

Ask staff: What issues or feelings does the story provoke in them? What kind of help do they think the teen wants? What interventions are likely to be most promising? Least effective? Why? How would you build trust with the teen writer? How have other adults failed the teen, and how might that affect his or her willingness to accept help? What other resources would be helpful to this teen, such as peer support, a mentor, counseling, family therapy, etc.

Resources on the Web

From time to time we will post Think About It questions on our website, www.youthcomm.org, to accompany stories in this and other Youth Communication books. We try out the questions with teens and post the ones that they find most effective. We'll also post lesson for some of the stories. Adults can use the questions and lessons in workshops.

Discussion Guide

Teachers and Staff:
How to Use This Book in Groups

When working with teens individually or in groups, using these stories can help young people face difficult issues in a way that feels safe to them. That's because talking about the issues in the stories usually feels safer to teens than talking about those same issues in their own lives. Addressing issues through the stories allows for some personal distance; they hit close to home, but not too close. Talking about them opens up a safe place for reflection. As teens gain confidence talking about the issues in the stories, they usually become more comfortable talking about those issues in their own lives.

Below are general questions that can help you lead discussions about the stories, which help teens and staff reflect on the issues in their own work and lives. In most cases you can read a story and conduct a discussion in one 45-minute session. Teens are usually happy to read the stories aloud, with each teen reading a paragraph or two. (Allow teens to pass if they don't want to read.) It takes 10-15 minutes to read a story straight through. However, it is often more effective to let workshop participants make comments and discuss the story as you go along. The workshop leader may even want to annotate her copy of the story beforehand with key questions.

If teens read the story ahead of time or silently, it's good to break the ice with a few questions that get everyone on the same page: Who is the main character? How old is she? What happened to her? How did she respond? Etc. Another good starting question is: "What stood out for you in the story?" Go around the room and let each person briefly mention one thing.

Then move on to open-ended questions, which encourage participants to think more deeply about what the writers were feeling, the choices they faced, and they actions they took. There are no right or wrong answers to the open-ended questions. Open-ended questions encourage participants to think about how the themes, emotions and choices in the stories relate to their own lives. Here are some examples of open-ended questions that we have found to be effective. You can use variations of these questions with almost any story in this book.

—What main problem or challenge did the writer face?

—What choices did the teen have in trying to deal with the problem?

—Which way of dealing with the problem was most effective for the teen? Why?

—What strengths, skills, or resources did the teen use to address the challenge?

—If you were in the writer's shoes, what would you have done?

—What could adults have done better to help this young person?

—What have you learned by reading this story that you didn't know before?

—What, if anything, will you do differently after reading this story?

—What surprised you in this story?

—Do you have a different view of this issue, or see a different way of dealing with it, after reading this story? Way or why not?

Credits

The stories in this book originally appeared in the following Youth Communication publications:

"The Crew from the Parking Lot," by Ferentz LaFargue, *New Youth Connections*, November 1992

"Becoming the Man My Dad Couldn't Be," by Rashad Evans, *New Youth Connections*, April 2008

"Camp Rising Sun: Where Guys Can Be Guys," by Jamal Greene, *New Youth Connections*, April 1995

"Getting Ghetto," by Fred Wagenhauser, *Represent*, March/April 2007

"Am I the Father?" by Anonymous, *New Youth Connections*, December 2003

"Getting Back My Heart," by Daniel Verzhbo, *Represent*, May/June 2008

"Becoming a Man, Jewish Style," by Chris Kanarick, *New Youth Connections*, May 1992

"A Girl Takes Control," by Troy Shawn Welcome, *New Youth Connections*, April 1994

"Wearing My True Colors," by Divine Strickland, *New Youth Connections*, March 2009

"From Shy Guy to Smooth Talker," by Juelz Long, *New Youth Connections*, January/February 2007

"Man With a Plan," by Michael Orr, *New Youth Connections*, January/February 2007

"My Secret Life As an Opera Singer," by Jonathan Maseng, *New Youth Connections*, March 2001

"Why Be a Thug?" by Tyrone Vaden, *Represent*, March/April 1999

"Skinniest Man in the Graveyard," by Anonymous, *New Youth Connections*, March 2008

"My Boy Wanted a Boyfriend" by Odé Manderson, *New Youth Connections*, May/June 2000

"Brokeback Breaks Hearts—and Stereotypes," by David Schmutzer, *New Youth Connections*, March 2006

"Messing Around's No Match for Love," by Christian Galindo, *New Youth Connections*, May/June 2002

"Barbershop Debates: A Rite of Passage," by David Etienne, *New Youth Connections*, May/June 2008

About
Youth Communication

Youth Communication, founded in 1980, is a nonprofit youth development program located in New York City whose mission is to teach writing, journalism, and leadership skills. The teenagers we train become writers for our websites and books and for two print magazines, *New Youth Connections*, a general-interest youth magazine, and *Represent*, a magazine by and for young people in foster care.

Each year, up to 100 young people participate in Youth Communication's school-year and summer journalism workshops where they work under the direction of full-time professional editors. Most are African American, Latino, or Asian, and many are recent immigrants. The opportunity to reach their peers with accurate portrayals of their lives and important self-help information motivates the young writers to create powerful stories.

Our goal is to run a strong youth development program in which teens produce high quality stories that inform and inspire their peers. Doing so requires us to be sensitive to the complicated lives and emotions of the teen participants while also providing an intellectually rigorous experience. We achieve that goal in the writing/teaching/editing relationship, which is the core of our program.

Our teaching and editorial process begins with discussions

between adult editors and the teen staff. In those meetings, the teens and the editors work together to identify the most important issues in the teens' lives and to figure out how those issues can be turned into stories that will resonate with teen readers.

Once story topics are chosen, students begin the process of crafting their stories. For a personal story, that means revisiting events in one's past to understand their significance for the future. For a commentary, it means developing a logical and persuasive point of view. For a reported story, it means gathering information through research and interviews. Students look inward and outward as they try to make sense of their experiences and the world around them and find the points of intersection between personal and social concerns. That process can take a few weeks or a few months. Stories frequently go through ten or more drafts as students work under the guidance of their editors, the way any professional writer does.

Many of the students who walk through our doors have uneven skills, as a result of poor education, living under extremely stressful conditions, or coming from homes where English is a second language. Yet, to complete their stories, students must successfully perform a wide range of activities, including writing and rewriting, reading, discussion, reflection, research, interviewing, and typing. They must work as members of a team and they must accept individual responsibility. They learn to provide constructive criticism, and to accept it. They engage in explorations of truthfulness, fairness, and accuracy. They meet deadlines. They must develop the audacity to believe that they have something important to say and the humility to recognize that saying it well is not a process of instant gratification. Rather, it usually requires a long, hard struggle through many discussions and much rewriting.

It would be impossible to teach these skills and dispositions as separate, disconnected topics, like grammar, ethics, or assertiveness. However, we find that students make rapid progress when they are learning skills in the context of an inquiry that is personally significant to them and that will benefit their peers.

When teens publish their stories—in *New Youth Connections* and *Represent*, on the web, and in other publications—they reach tens of thousands of teen and adult readers. Teachers, counselors, social workers, and other adults circulate the stories to young people in their classes and out-of-school youth programs. Adults tell us that teens in their programs—including many who are ordinarily resistant to reading—clamor for the stories. Teen readers report that the stories give them information they can't get anywhere else, and inspire them to reflect on their lives and open lines of communication with adults.

Writers usually participate in our program for one semester, though some stay much longer. Years later, many of them report that working here was a turning point in their lives—that it helped them acquire the confidence and skills that they needed for success in college and careers. Scores of our graduates have overcome tremendous obstacles to become journalists, writers, and novelists. They include National Book Award finalist Edwidge Danticat, novelist Ernesto Quinonez, writer Veronica Chambers and *New York Times* reporter Rachel Swarns. Hundreds more are working in law, business, and other careers. Many are teachers, principals, and youth workers, and several have started nonprofit youth programs themselves and work as mentors—helping another generation of young people develop their skills and find their voices.

Youth Communication is a nonprofit educational corporation. Contributions are gratefully accepted and are tax deductible to the fullest extent of the law.

To make a contribution, or for information about our publications and programs, including our catalog of over 100 books and curricula for hard-to-reach teens, see www.youthcomm.org

About The Editors

Al Desetta has been an editor of Youth Communication's two teen magazines, *Foster Care Youth United* (now known as *Represent*) and *New Youth Connections*. He was also an instructor in Youth Communication's juvenile prison writing program. In 1991, he became the organization's first director of teacher development, working with high school teachers to help them produce better writers and student publications.

Prior to working at Youth Communication, Desetta directed environmental education projects in New York City public high schools and worked as a reporter.

He has a master's degree in English literature from City College of the City University of New York and a bachelor's degree from the State University of New York at Binghamton, and he was a Revson Fellow at Columbia University for the 1990-91 academic year.

He is the editor of many books, including several other Youth Communication anthologies: *The Heart Knows Something Different: Teenage Voices from the Foster Care System, The Struggle to Be Strong*, and *The Courage to Be Yourself*. He is currently a freelance editor.

Keith Hefner co-founded Youth Communication in 1980 and has directed it ever since. He is the recipient of the Luther P. Jackson Education Award from the New York Association of Black Journalists and a MacArthur Fellowship. He was also a Revson Fellow at Columbia University.

Laura Longhine is the editorial director at Youth Communication. She edited *Represent*, Youth Communication's magazine by and for youth in foster care, for three years, and has written for a variety of publications. She has a BA in English from Tufts University and an MS in Journalism from Columbia University.

More Helpful Books
From Youth Comunication

The Struggle to Be Strong: True Stories by Teens About Overcoming Tough Times. Foreword by Veronica Chambers. Help young people identify and build on their own strengths with 30 personal stories about resiliency. (Free Spirit)

Starting With "I": Personal Stories by Teenagers. "Who am I and who do I want to become?" Thirty-five stories examine this question through the lens of race, ethnicity, gender, sexuality, family, and more. Increase this book's value with the free Teacher's Guide, available from youthcomm.org. (Youth Communication)

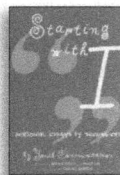

Real Stories, Real Teens. Inspire teens to read and recognize their strengths with this collection of 26 true stories by teens. The young writers describe how they overcame significant challenges and stayed true to themselves. Also includes the first chapters from three novels in the Bluford Series. (Youth Communication)

The Courage to Be Yourself: True Stories by Teens About Cliques, Conflicts, and Overcoming Peer Pressure. In 26 first-person stories, teens write about their lives with searing honesty. These stories will inspire young readers to reflect on their own lives, work through their problems, and help them discover who they really are. (Free Spirit)

Out With It: Gay and Straight Teens Write About Homosexuality. Break stereotypes and provide support with this unflinching look at gay life from a teen's perspective. With a focus on urban youth, this book also includes several heterosexual teens' transformative experiences with gay peers. (Youth Communication)

Things Get Hectic: Teens Write About the Violence That Surrounds Them. Violence is commonplace in many teens' lives, be it bullying, gangs, dating, or family relationships. Hear the experiences of victims, perpetrators, and witnesses through more than 50 real-world stories. (Youth Communication)

From Dropout to Achiever: Teens Write About School. Help teens overcome the challenges of graduating, which may involve overcoming family problems, bouncing back from a bad semester, or even dropping out for a time. These teens show how they achieve academic success. (Youth Communication)

My Secret Addiction: Teens Write About Cutting. These true accounts of cutting, or self-mutilation, offer a window into the personal and family situations that lead to this secret habit, and show how teens can get the help they need. (Youth Communication)

Sticks and Stones: Teens Write About Bullying. Shed light on bullying, as told from the perspectives of the bully, the victim, and the witness. These stories show why bullying occurs, the harm it causes, and how it might be prevented. (Youth Communication)

Through Thick and Thin: Teens Write About Obesity, Eating Disorders, and Self Image. Help teens who struggle with obesity, eating disorders, and body weight issues. These stories show the pressures teens face when they are confronted by unrealistic standards for physical appearance, and how emotions can affect the way we eat. (Youth Communication)

To order these and other books, go to:
www.youthcomm.org
or call 212-279-0708 x115

www.ingramcontent.com/pod-product-compliance
Lightning Source LLC
Chambersburg PA
CBHW051738090426
42738CB00010B/2308